We start on our travels by train [Mary, Dick, Helen, Bob, Jack, and Edith]

CARPENTERS' JOURNEY CLUB TRAVELS

THE
WAYS WE TRAVEL

BY

FRANCES CARPENTER, F.R.G.S.

AMERICAN BOOK COMPANY

NEW YORK   CINCINNATI   CHICAGO   BOSTON   ATLANTA

PREFACE

The Ways We Travel, one of Carpenters' "Journey Club Travels," is the story of the adventures of the children of the Journey Club as they find out about the different means by which man and his messages are taken from one place to another. At their first meeting the importance of transportation and communication in the daily lives of the children is brought out and the early history of the two subjects is briefly summarized. The new travels begin with a fast trip around the world, during which children ride in jinrikishas in Japan, in sedan chairs and wheelbarrows in China, upon elephants in India, and in strange vehicles in other far-away lands. Two of the Club members, dressed in costume, then tell of transportation in early settlements of America, tracing its development from the days of the Indian trails and birch-bark canoes, through the times of George Washington, with their gayly-painted coaches, and post riders on horseback.

During a tramp to a picnicking spot in the country near by they learn about travel on foot; and winter visits to Michigan, Eskimo-land, and Alaska give them experiences of travel over ice and snow in sleds drawn by horses, reindeer, and dogs. A day on the farm of one of the Journey Club members introduces the children to their friend, the horse, while an old letter from a trunk in the attic paints for them a vivid picture of the period when the bicycle was a favorite means of getting about.

To find out about railroads, the Journey Club visits the Fair of the Iron Horse where the children witness the various steps in the evolution of the modern giant locomotive. They go through a locomotive works near Philadelphia, and then travel from New York to Chicago on a fast express train, observing carefully the features of a modern Pullman sleeper, and talking with a railroad builder of the task of laying a railroad and of the importance to the world of railway freight service. A street car takes the Club to the street railway car-barns, where its members discuss city transportation with the superintendent, and from whence they return in a modern motor bus. This is followed by a trip to see a motion picture which deals with the elevated railways, the subways, and the Holland Tunnel in the city of New York.

A journey to Detroit in interurban motor buses brings out the important part that automobiles play in our modern life, and a day in a huge factory shows how an automobile is put together. Good roads and road building form the subject of another investigation. The children arrange an original pageant that sets forth the basic facts in the history of shipping. They follow this with a voyage across the ocean in a giant steamship, during which they talk with the engineer and the captain, and learn how ships are built. They fly in a great plane from their own city to the next airport on the mail

and passenger air line; they watch the telegram they are sending being started out over the wires; and they personally inspect their own telephone exchange. A radio talk from a big broadcasting station gives them an insight into the mechanism of this means of communication as well as a glimpse of some of our latest modern marvels, television, telephotography, and transoceanic telephoning.

Throughout the book the idea of the division of labor is stressed. Emphasis is laid upon the vast amount of effort involved in providing for the children the conveniences of their daily life, and the necessity of each doing his share in the work of the world.

Care has been taken to deal only with those phases of transportation and communication which are within the range of the child's comprehension. The study is not formalized. It is the story of the real experiences of real children. The Journey Club and the men and the women whom it encounters on its travels live for the young reader. The illusion is made more realistic in that certain of the Club members are mentioned by name throughout the series, and their photographs appear in almost every chapter.

The value of the Club organization and the desirability of the maintenance of the museum cannot be overestimated. Suggestions to teachers concerning the working out of the project problems and the arrangement of the museum will be found both in the text and on pages 292 to 296. An index is provided on pages 297 and 298.

In the publication of this volume of Carpenter's "Journey Club Travels," *The Ways We Travel*, the author wishes to make grateful acknowledgment of the help received through suggestions and comments from the following:

Messrs. Richard Waterman, Charles W. Stark, A. T. Stewart, and N. Sumner Myrick, of the Transportation and Communication Department of the United States Chamber of Commerce, Washington, D. C.; Mr. Pyke Johnson, Secretary, National Automobile Chamber of Commerce, Washington, D. C.; Mr. C. L. Doggett, United States Shipping Board; Mr. Edwin F. Hill, Chesapeake and Potomac Telephone Company; Mr. A. F. Taff, Western Union Telegraph Company; and the Bureau of Public Roads, Washington, D. C.

While many of the illustrations are from negatives made by the author, these have been supplemented by photographs from the following sources: Harley-Davidson Motor Company, New York Central Lines, Baltimore and Ohio Railroad Company, Pennsylvania Railroad Company, The French Line, United States Lines, International Mercantile Marine Company, Chesapeake and Potomac Telephone Company, Western Union Telegraph Company, Baldwin Locomotive Works, General Electric Company, Royal Mail Steam Packet Company, Ford Motor Company, National Automobile Chamber of Commerce, General Motors Corporation, B. F. Mahoney Aircraft Corporation, Loening Aëronautical Engineering Corporation, Curtiss Aëroplane and Motor Company, Russell Parachute Company, Keystone View Company, Boeing Air Transport, Inc., Sprague

Publishing Company, Embry-Riddle Company, N. W. Ayer and Son, National Broadcasting Company, Jenkins Laboratories, L. C. Handy, Barrett Company, Portland Cement Company, Washington Rapid Transit Company, Bureau of Aëronautics, Navy Department, Radio Corporation of America, Smithsonian National Museum, Boy Scouts of America, Atlantic Transport Line, U. S. Bureau of Public Roads, U. S. Department of Agriculture, White Star Line, Capital Traction Company, Edmonston, Austin Company, and Miss Amelia Earhart.

The photographs of the Journey Club children, together with a number of others, were made by I. Pridgeon, Washington, D. C.

Permission to use "Columbus" was granted by the Harr Wagner Publishing Company, publishers of Joaquin Miller's *Complete Poems*: acknowledgment is due also to Houghton Mifflin Company and *The Ohio Motorist* for permission to use copyrighted material.

CONTENTS

CHAPTER 1

CHAPTER 2

CHAPTER 3

CHAPTER 4

CHAPTER 5

CHAPTER 6

CHAPTER 7

CHAPTER 8

CHAPTER 9

CONTENTS

CONTENTS

THE WAYS WE TRAVEL

CHAPTER 1

OUR JOURNEY CLUB MUSEUM

"This is our Museum!" says Mary, who is president of the Journey Club for this year. She is showing our new members the interesting curios we have picked up on the travels which we have made to find out about our food, our clothes, and our houses.

"Those rice stalks grew in far-off Japan," she explains, pointing to one of the food exhibits. "That coconut in the corner was sent to us by our friend, Benito, who lives in the Philippine Islands. That lump of rock salt was given to us by a workman in a salt mine in Louisiana. Look at this cocoon! We got it during our

Traveling by camel

visit to Kito-San's silkworms in Japan. And this ivory button was once part of the tusk of an elephant of the African jungle. That white stone is a bit of marble from Italy, while the Oriental rug in this picture was woven in Persia."

"How many countries you must have visited!" cries one of our new members.

"Yes, our motto is 'to find out,'" says Jack. "And in order to find out about all these things we have had to make many, many long trips, for, as you can see, these exhibits come from every part of the globe."

"But where are the exhibits

that tell how you traveled on those journeys of yours?" another new member asks. "Don't you have some that show how all these things were brought together here in our Museum? I should like to know about the

Great ships carry us over the oceans

ships and the trains, the motor cars and the airplanes that carried you and your curios from one place to another."

There is a silence. Mary looks at Jack, and Dick looks at Bob. We do not know quite what to say. We truly enjoyed our trips in the automobiles and the trains that carried us so swiftly over the land, and on the ships that bore us so pleasantly across the broad oceans. We remember how we rode on horses and camels and

sure-footed donkeys, and we shall never forget our flights through the clouds in whirring airplanes. But we have been so intent on our foods, our clothes, and our houses that we have not taken time to find out about the many different ways in which we have traveled.

"I know what we should do," Helen cries out, her eyes shining brightly in her excitement. "We should make some new journeys to find out about the ways we travel. Let us travel again in trains and in automobiles, upon steamships and in airplanes! Let us see just how they are made and who runs them for us! Let us find out too about all the queer ways in which people of other lands travel and about the long journeys that are made by the things we use every day."

"Good! Good!" we cry together. We are delighted at the thought of more wonderful Journey Club Travels.

"Some of these curios of ours were sent to us by our friends of far-away lands," Dick says thoughtfully. "We can get most things we need without actually going to the places where they are made. All we have to do is to order them sent to us by mail, freight, or express. I think we should also find out how we can send such orders to

Why We Need Ways of Travel

Just think what would happen if there were to be a world strike that would cause all means of travel to halt. As Mary was explaining about our Museum, we saw how many of the things that we use every day are brought to

We need steam shovels and railroads to bring us our coal

people in other parts of the world. I should like to know about our telephones and telegraphs, about our cables, and about messages that are flashed through the air by radio."

We take a vote. Every one present cries, "Aye," as loud as he can. It is quickly decided that we shall follow these suggestions made by Helen and Dick.

us from far, far away. Without ships or trains and other means to carry them from one place to the other, we could have but few of these comforts. We should have to get on with what we could make in our own town. And even then we should have no machinery to help us, for the coal and the other things we must have to run the factories and mills could not be brought to us without trains, ships, and trucks.

The only food and clothes we should have would be those we could make by the work of our hands, from such materials as we could find in our own neighborhood. These materials would

Wild ducks fly swiftly

not last long. We should soon have eaten up all of our food. Our clothes would wear out. Our houses would tumble to pieces for lack of materials to repair them. At last we should be living as uncomfortably as did the very first settlers who came to America when our land was a wilderness.

What Journey Club member can run as fast as a dog, or a cat, or a horse? Indeed, most of the animals can go from one place to another faster than man. The birds of the air, the fishes under the sea, and the wild creatures of the forest can almost all move more quickly than we when we must depend upon our own legs.

Mother Nature wisely takes care that her animal children shall be able to run, swim, or fly swiftly enough to get out of harm's way. She takes care of her human children by quite other means. She gives us our brains and the power to think for ourselves. With these tools, men have invented wonderful ways of traveling with speed from one place to another. Indeed, when we think that a train or an automobile can go fifteen times as fast as a man can walk, and that an airplane will fly nearly three times as fast as a train can go, our ways of travel seem almost miracles. To-day, by means of such modern miracles, we can comfortably visit all parts of the world. If we had to walk, we could never go very far from our own homes.

How Strong-as-a-Lion Traveled

In our other Journey Club Travels we have found out about a boy whom we call Strong-as-a-Lion. He lived long ago when there were savages. We believe that many people then went almost naked and that they dwelt in caves in the rocks. Strong-as-a-Lion's wee baby brother was perhaps one of the very first travelers to go from one place to another without using his legs. His shaggy-haired mother carried him in her arms wherever she went. Later she made him a little hammock of fur skin which she slung over her back. In this way her baby could travel in comfort and ease whenever the family went on a journey. Some American Indians, Eskimos, and people of other lands still carry their papooses in much the same way.

Indian girl carrying her baby brother

At first Strong-as-a-Lion's father and his big brothers brought home on their backs the beasts they killed for food in the forest. Or they slung them over a stick which they bore between them on their shoulders.

At last one of them said to the other: "Let us take this forked branch and lay the beast on it. Then we can drag it back to our cave without tiring our backs."

Their idea worked well. After that they brought home all their game in this fashion. Sometimes when the men were not looking, Strong-as-a-Lion jumped on the branch, too. But he had only a short ride before they felt his weight and he was driven off by a blow from his father's great fist.

What rejoicing there was in these savage homes when a wild ox or a wild horse was caught! The cave-people soon found out that such creatures could be tamed and made to carry their burdens. When game became

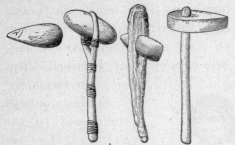

Tools made of wood and stone

scarce about the cave where Strong-as-a-Lion lived, his family would move on to another. At first this was easy. They had nothing to carry but the fur skins on their backs. Later on they learned to shape tools of stone. The men made more and more clubs and bows and arrows. They then found that their moving was not so simple as it had been in the past. Remembering how he had dragged his game home on a forked branch, the savage father cut down two

An Indian family traveling by drag cart

straight young trees. He stripped off the branches. By tying crosspieces across one end of them, he made a rude framework. To the other end of this he hitched his tame horse, letting the end with the framework lie on the ground. He found that by this drag cart that would lift the frame from the ground and that would turn as the cart moved. It was from such a roller as this that man got his first idea of a wheel. And it was the invention of the wheel that paved the way for the coming of our wagons and

The drag cart was given wheels

means he was able to drag quite a load to his next cave dwelling place.

It may have been Strong-as-a-Lion himself or one of his children who later discovered that a round log placed under a heavy object would roll and make it move more easily. Perhaps this gave him the idea of using a roller on his carriages. It is because we know about wheels that we now may have the bicycles and automobiles, the trains, ships, and airplanes we ride in to-day.

The Very First Ship

One afternoon as Strong-as-a-Lion's father stood fishing on the bank of a stream, the trunk

Making a dugout by hollowing out a log

of a fallen tree floated slowly past him.

"If the water is strong enough to hold up that tree," he said to himself in his queer cave-man speech, "perhaps it would bear my weight as well. Riding on a log like that, I could travel far without tiring."

He ran along the bank. Catching hold of the log, he balanced himself upon it. To his delight the log did not sink. He shouted to his family to come and see him as he rode in state down the stream. But getting back to his home was quite another matter. He did not now have the rushing current to carry him along. At first he did not know what to do, but he thought and he thought, and he soon saw a way out. He found a tall pole that would reach to the bottom of the river. With this he pushed his log back up the stream until at last he came to the spot from which he had set forth. By tying many such logs together he invented a raft that would carry his whole family at one time.

Later he learned that he could hollow out a log so that he could squat in it more comfortably as he paddled up and down stream. In this dugout, as such boats are called, he had also room to take with him Strong-as-a-Lion and the things he needed for his

An early sailboat

Without wheels we could not have our fine automobiles

hunting and fishing. A hollow log like this was perhaps one of the very first boats.

Another man of these early times found out how to raise over his boat a hide stretched on a wood framework, so as to make the breezes blow him from one part of the river to the other. It is in this way we think sails were first invented.

How We Travel To-day

It is now many thousands of years since Strong-as-a-Lion sailed in his hollow log boat or rode on his crude drag cart. Each year man has learned better how to move himself and his goods from one place to the other. Those first drags and their rollers became carts and wagons. The wagons were made into fine carriages drawn by teams of prancing horses, and these were followed by carriages pulled by steam engines. At last there were born the fast express trains that fly over the land at the speed of a mile a minute, and the beautiful automobiles that carry us so comfortably over roads as smooth as a floor.

Strong-as-a-Lion's crude dug-outs in the passing of years became sailing vessels. Then came steam and the vessels gradually grew into the giant steamships of steel that now cross the vast oceans in so short a time. The latest and greatest of all our modern miracles of travel are the bird-like airplanes and great dirigibles that soar up out of sight into the clouds.

But we shall find that many peoples of the world still use ways

The Journey Club watch a steam locomotive [Edith, Bob, Mary, Jack, Helen, and Dick]

of travel almost as crude as those of savage times. We shall see them bearing great burdens on their own backs, and riding in log canoes and rude boats of skin. We shall meet others who use elephants, oxen, donkeys, and dogs, and even men, to carry them.

As we go about on our new journeys we shall see again how our comfort depends on the work of our fellow men. We shall talk with the engineers on the trains, with the pilots of the airplanes, and with the captains and the crews of the steamships and river boats. Thousands of men and women choose this way of earning their living and of doing their share in the work of the world. They will tell us that ways of travel are called *transportation*.

As Dick suggested, we shall discover how our telephone, telegraph, and radio have come to us. We shall hear of the people of early times who lit fires on the mountains to signal by or used fast runners to take messages to their neighbors. We shall learn that the ways we send such messages are called *communication*.

"Are you ready?" asks Mary, when she has written down in our record book the names of all the new members. We hope your name is among them. We want you to join our Journey Club if you do not already belong, and we want you to come along with us as we set forth on our trips to find out about the ways we travel.

CHAPTER 2

ODD WAYS OF TRAVEL IN FAR–AWAY LANDS

Our bags are packed. Our trunks have already left our San Francisco hotel. We are ready to sail. We have decided that our first Journey Club trip shall be to find out about some of the queer means of travel used by our friends of far-away lands. We wish to visit so many countries that we shall be able to stop in each one only long enough to make a few trips with the boys and the girls who live there, and to collect photographs for the shelves of our Museum.

If wishes came true

"I wish we had a Magic Carpet," says Bob. "Then we could go from one place to another in the wink of an eye." We all remember the old tale about the Indian Prince and his wonderful rug. He had only to sit on it and wish himself in a certain place. And lo, he was there! But alas, the days of the Magic Carpet are no more. The Journey Club will have to depend upon railways and great ocean steamships for its tour of the world.

Our time on shipboard passes quickly. In a little more than a week, almost before we know it, we have crossed the wide Pacific Ocean. As we near the island of Japan, we send a radio message to our Japanese friends with whom we have already taken so many interesting trips.

come. They say they would like nothing better than to take us for a ride in true Japanese fashion.

We Ride in a Jinrikisha

What a bustle there is just outside the pier! Street cars are

We see a group of jinrikishas

"See, there is Taro!" Jack cries, as we steam up to the dock at Yokohama.

"And Haruko-San, too," Mary says. We rush down the gangplank. Soon we are all talking and laughing together. The Japanese boy and girl are delighted to hear why we have

rumbling by. Automobiles are sounding their horns. Rude wagons are creaking past under their heavy loads of rice and silk. And above all this din we hear some strange voices calling out, "Rik'sha, Rik'sha."

Taro leads us to some odd little carriages. They are *jinrikishas*.

In spite of the many fine automobiles that whizz through the streets of the Japanese cities, some of the travel is still done in these tiny two-wheeled carriages drawn by yellow-skinned men.

jinrikisha. Our hikis step in between the narrow shafts. Each one throws a strap across his shoulders and fastens its loops to the ends of the shafts. He grasps the crosspiece between the shafts

A Japanese lady traveling by jinrikisha

Taro talks with some of the runners whom he calls *hikis*. These odd little taxis have no meters to count the distance traveled and tell us how much we must pay. That is why he thinks it best to make a fixed price before we set out.

We each take our seat in a

with his strong yellow fingers. With curious cries, the hikis all start off together. These runners are lean men, clad in black trousers and loose blue cotton coats. On the back of each coat we see markings in red and white. Taro says they are the license numbers of these strange taxi-men.

How quick and strong our man-horses are! We roll through the streets at a great speed. Jack's hiki speaks a little English. He tells him he can pull his rik'sha for thirty or forty miles in a day and not be at all tired at the end of his journey. He always carries an extra pair of sandals tied to his shafts, for the straw shoes he wears do not last long.

Look at that jinrikisha we are passing now! It is big enough for two persons. Two Japanese girls are sitting in it chattering and giggling as they ride along. See this fat man coming toward us! He is so heavy that it takes three men

A Korean with his jiggy

to pull his jinrikisha. The two extra hikis are helping by means of stout straps fastened to the sides of the shafts. Three runners are used also when a traveler wishes to make greater speed.

Taro tells us that it was an American missionary named Goble who invented the jinrikisha. He says that this light little carriage can go over roads which are not smooth enough for automobiles. Many of Taro's people are too poor to afford to ride even in a jinrikisha. They travel long distances on foot, and we see men bearing great loads on their shoulders and backs. Here comes a cart pushed by a man, and there goes a wagon drawn by oxen shod with straw shoes.

"Oh, it is raining," Edith calls out, as a shower comes up. The hikis let down the shafts and pull up the hoods of our jinrikishas. These remind us of the hoods on baby carriages, for they are really quite small. But they keep off the rain and we are brought back to our ship without getting wet. Our runners show us the lanterns of oiled paper which they hang on the shafts when the dark comes. These lanterns are pretty, but we do not think they are so useful as the electric headlights on our automobiles at home.

A Korean Jiggy

Our next stop is in Korea, or Chosen, as it is called now that it belongs to Japan. The Korean roads are so bad in many places that no vehicle can be used. In some parts of the country where the railroads do not run, the highways are often only narrow paths. Travelers must go on foot or on horseback. We talk with the Korean porters who carry most of the loads in this little country. They show us their *jiggies*. These are strong frameworks of wood which they fasten on their backs. Here is a porter just loading his jiggy. The wooden frame rests on the ground. It is propped up with a forked stick. The porter puts a huge trunk upon it.

Koreans carry great loads on their jiggies

He slips his arms through the padded loops on its sides, raises it easily up from the ground, and trots off down the path.

One of the porters asks Mary if she would not like to take a ride on his jiggy. He says in the past many people were carried from place to place in this way. His jiggy has pieces of wood nailed upon it so as to form a crude seat. We shout with laughter as Mary sits on the jiggy. The porter stoops and lifts her to a perch on his back, high above us. He runs down the road and then brings her back. She thanks him as she jumps down from her queer seat, but she whispers to us that it was not at all comfortable.

Trips with Ah Chee

Our stay in China lasts for several days. We have as our guide our young friend, Ah Chee, who plans a number of trips for us. Here in Shanghai, as in Yokohama, we find many street cars, automobiles, and jinrikishas. We see wagons and carts pulled by groups of men, and by horses and oxen. But many of the streets of the old Chinese cities are so narrow that even a jinrikisha cannot make its way through them. Standing in the middle of one of these old streets, we can almost touch the houses on either side with our finger

Much of Korea's goods is carried by man

tips. We can hardly believe that any vehicle can get through them until Ah Chee takes us to see a sedan chair.

"It is just a chair inside a small house," says Bob as we look at the sedan. Its framework is light. It is covered with cloth. Some of the finest sedan chairs have walls of silk and cushions of satin. Ah Chee points out the tiny windows at the side with their little straw shutters. The open front of the sedan serves as a door. The Chinese boy tells Dick how to back in and sit down in the

Many Chinese travel in sedan chairs

chair. Then he asks the two bearers to show us how they carry it. There are two long poles that run along the sides of the sedan chair. The men stand between these. Lifting the chair, they run a few steps to show us how easy it is.

The Useful Wheelbarrow

Squeak! Squeak! Squeeeeeaaaa-k!

"What is that dreadful noise?" Helen asks, putting her hands over her ears. We are again on a wide street, in all kinds of traffic. Ah Chee laughs.

"That is a wheelbarrow," he says. "You must surely have a ride on a wheelbarrow, for in many parts of our land that is the chief means of travel." He stops the wheelbarrow man. By paying him a few cents, he persuades him to unload his packages and to give us each a ride. We have never seen a wheelbarrow just like this. Its one great wheel is in the very center, and a frame is built above it and out on each

In China many people ride on wheelbarrows

Riding on a Chinese cart

side. There is room for four of us to ride at a time. Helen and Bob sit on one side and Edith and Jack take seats on the other.

The man has a strap over his shoulders to help him bear the weight. With a push and a grunt he starts us off on our ride. Creak! Creak! Creak! How uncomfortable it is! We do not envy the Chinese traveler who must depend on such means of getting about.

"You see, many of our roads are so poor that we cannot use automobiles upon them," says Ah Chee. "Sometimes in the coun-try the highways are little more than footpaths. Or perhaps they may be roads of soft earth with a narrow paved way about a foot wide built through the center. The farmers often find that using the wheelbarrow is the best way to bring their wares to market over such roads."

Another means of travel which we try with Ah Chee is the two-wheeled Chinese cart drawn by a small horse. Its roof is of blue cotton, and its huge wheels sing almost as loud a song as the creaking wheelbarrow. It is so small that we have to sit cross-legged inside, and we soon grow tired of holding the same position. Now and then we perch outside on the shafts to rest ourselves. After a short trip out into the country, an elephant. By good fortune we arrive at a large city on the day of a festival. The rajah, whose palace we visit there, has several fine elephants. He allows us to

An elephant ready for the festival procession

our very bones ache, for these carts have no springs.

On the Back of an Elephant

The next stage of our world tour brings us to India. Here we have a ride on the back of watch one of the great beasts led out and harnessed for the festival procession. Gay velvet blankets embroidered with gold are draped over his sides. A little house with seats for his riders is strapped on his broad back. Such little houses are called *howdahs*. They are hung with bright silks, and soft cushions lie on their seats.

Near by are a number of men dressed in white suits with red sashes around their waists. Their up into the howdah. We clutch the sides of our seats as the elephant rises again to his feet. We are jolted this way and that as he goes round the courtyard with his queer lurching step. One of

Elephants do the work of men and machines in Burmese lumber yards

long black hair is hidden by turbans of white cotton cloth. We find that they are the *mahouts*, which means the drivers of the elephants.

One mahout strikes the elephant lightly on his knees and makes him kneel down. A little ladder is placed against his side. The mahout beckons us to climb the mahouts sits on the elephant's head, just behind his ears. He guides him with cries and with taps of his long stick. Another mahout walks slowly in front.

From our journeys to find out about the houses we live in we remember the elephants that worked so well in the lumber yards and the forests of India and

A great caravan of camels traveling over the Sahara

Burmah. We should like to stay to see an elephant hunt in the jungle here, but we shall not have time.

Travel in the Desert

Hassan and Hada, our two friends of the African desert, are our next hosts. We hire camels to carry us out to the oasis where they live. It takes us some time to get used to the motion of these swaying beasts. At first we feel almost seasick. We do not wonder the camel is called "the ship of the desert."

Ever since any one can remember the camel has been the chief means of travel in desert lands. His stomach is so made that he can store away enough water to last him many days. A horse has to drink often. He would die if he had to travel far into the desert.

Now and then we pass an automobile plowing its way through the sands. We wonder why they do not have railroads here in the desert. But our very first sand storm shows us the reason. The winds blow the sand hills about

Benito rides upon a carabao

boxes of fruit may even find their way into the stores of our own town. The camels of this caravan are of many colors. Some are light tan. Others are gray, brown, or rusty black. Their drivers are clad in loose white cotton robes, and they wear cloths over their heads to protect them from the sun. These camels are freight camels. They travel only about three miles an hour. Our camels are riding-camels called

from place to place. Rails would soon be covered over and the trains could not run. Then too, there are not enough people who live in the desert to make a railroad worth while.

Here comes a caravan. How many camels there are! There must be more than one hundred. They walk nose to tail, one just behind the other. Their backs are loaded with dates from the oasis where Hassan lives. They may be going to the very steamer upon which we are traveling, and these

Traveling by chair in the hills of the Philippines

In Belgium dogs draw carts about the streets

meharis. They go much faster than the freight camels. The camel has sad looking eyes. He often cries out while he is being loaded.

Why Good Roads Are Important

During our world tour we see other strange means of transportation. In many places men and women carry heavy burdens on their heads. In Madeira the roads are of smooth cobblestones. There some of the carriages have iron runners instead of wheels. They are drawn by oxen. When coming down a cobblestone hill, the oxen are often unhitched and the car coasts to the bottom all by itself. In Belgium and Holland dogs are sometimes used instead of horses or donkeys, and in the Philippine

Islands we see that our friend, Benito, rides upon a strange ox called a *carabao*.

But in all the lands we visit, we find that the ways in which the people travel depend on their roads. Where the roads are good, they can use carriages and horses and automobiles. They can thus travel comfortably. Where the roads are poor, they must go about on foot or on horseback, on oxen or on camels, in creaking wheelbarrows, or in chairs borne by donkeys or by men. Where the roads are better, they can travel farther and can have more of the comforts of life brought to their homes. It is always true that the countries which are the most comfortable to live in are those which have the best roads.

CHAPTER 3

THE TRAVELS OF PATIENCE TRUE AND JOHN ADAMS

"Members of the Journey Club, we bid you welcome to our meeting to-day." Mary speaks in a prim tone. She makes a deep curtsy. Bob, who stands beside her, bows low before us as we come in. Mary is clad in a dress of dark homespun that falls to her ankles. She has a white kerchief and a cap that covers her hair.

"My name is Patience True," she explains to our new members. "I lived long, long ago. My family came to America with some of the first white settlers. Those early set-

In Colonial days

tlements belonged to England and to other countries of Europe. They were called *colonies*. Those times are often spoken of as Colonial days."

"This is John Adams," Mary says, leading Bob forward. "He is an American boy who lived when George Washington was President of the United States." Bob is dressed in a long coat and a pair of knee breeches. He wears a white wig whose little pigtail of hair is wrapped round and round with a piece of black ribbon.

"We are to tell you of the ways

people traveled in Colonial days and in the days when our nation was very young," John Adams says, smiling. "Patience True will speak first, for she journeyed over our land more than one hundred and fifty years before I was born."

We all find seats in Helen's living room where we are meeting. Patience True takes her place in the center of our circle and begins her story.

In the Footsteps of the Indians

"When my family came to America, the land along the seacoast was a wilderness of dense forests. There were no roads. There were no real bridges. Carriages and wagons were unknown. At first we stayed close to our log homes. But little by little we found that we needed to travel about in our own neighborhood. My father and brothers had to go out in the woods to hunt, and my mother and I went now and then to call on our friends.

"I was delighted when my mother took me with her to visit my aunt who lived on the other side of the forest. The trip was always exciting. We trudged over the narrow trails that had

We crossed the streams on logs

been made by the Indians in going from their camping grounds to the springs for water. When we came to a stream, we often had to wade through it or hop from one to another of its flat stepping stones. Or we balanced ourselves carefully as we walked over the log that had been laid across the rushing waters as a kind of rude foot bridge.

"My father and the other men of our village soon made many new paths. First they went through the forests with their sharp axes. They chopped slivers of bark from the trees along the way they wanted the path to go.

Our fathers blazed the trails

They called this blazing the trail. The white blazes on the trees stood out clearly in the dim light of the woods so that others who came after them could find their way easily. They threw the stones out of the path and they cut down the bushes. By tramp-ing over and over the same route day after day, they soon had a smooth pathway wide enough for a man to pass through on foot or riding on horseback."

Dugouts and Canoes

. "All our long trips were made on the water," says Patience True. "We built our villages close to the rivers and bays so that we could go from one to the other in dug-outs and canoes such as we saw the Indians using.

"How proud we were of those first boats of ours! You see, some of the Indians in our neighborhood were peaceful and friendly. In ex-change for glass beads and other things which we had brought over from England, they carved us a dugout from a huge log. First they had to find just the right kind of pine tree. They hollowed its trunk out by burning and scraping away the part that was not needed.

"Our first dugout was about twenty feet long and three feet wide. It took our Indian friends almost three weeks to make it. Crude boats like these were the ones the Indians knew best. They were amazed when they first saw the Good Ship *Mayflower* in which we Pilgrims landed on Plymouth Rock. They thought of course it had been hollowed out of a giant tree, larger than any they had ever seen.

"It was an Indian who later taught my father to make a birch-bark canoe. In Longfellow's beautiful poem, *Hiawatha*, you may read how such a canoe was put together. This is one verse of the poem:

"'Thus the Birch Canoe was builded
    In the valley, by the river,
    In the bosom of the forest;
    And the forest's life was in it,
    All its mystery and its magic,
    All the lightness of the birch-tree,
    All the toughness of the cedar,
    All the larch's supple sinews;
    And it floated on the river
    Like a yellow leaf in autumn.'

"Our birch-bark canoe would hold six persons in comfort. The Indians had even larger ones. Some of their war canoes had room for twenty or thirty Indian braves and for their bows and arrows as well. We traveled a great deal in our birch-bark canoe. It was so light, it was easy for my father to carry it over the land when we had to go from one

Hunting in a birch-bark canoe

stream to another. With long strokes of our paddles we soon learned to send our birch-bark craft speeding over the water.

"Once I went with my father to the town of Boston. When we came to the Charles River we found there a canoe ferry. The ferry man charged us six cents apiece to paddle us across. There was a horseback rider who crossed at the same time. He rode in the canoe holding on tight to the bridle of his horse, which plunged into the water and swam after the boat. In this way the rider did not have to pay for the horse. Sometimes such ferries carried a horse in two canoes. The animal's front feet were placed in one canoe and its hind feet in another. The boats were fastened firmly together so the horse could be ferried safely across."

Patience Rides upon Horseback

"But the best way of all to travel in my time was on the back of a horse." Patience True's face beams as she goes on with her story. "My father's brother in England sent us a horse. It was brought across the ocean in a sailing vessel. Most of the horses the colonists used came in this way from England, Holland, or Spain. When Father set out on horseback, I often climbed up behind him. I felt very grown-up as I sat perched on the *pillion*, a padded cushion that was strapped to the horse's back just behind Father's saddle. My feet barely touched the little wood platform that hung over its side and served as a foot-rest. When the horse trotted, I clutched Father's coat with all my might for fear I should be jolted off into the path.

"When Mother and Brother Jonathan wished to go along too, we all used the same horse. But of course not at the same

Riding on a pillion

time. Father and I would ride for a short distance. Then we would get down, tie our horse to a tree, and go forward on foot. Mother and Jonathan had started out from the house walking. They would soon reach the spot where our horse was tied. They would climb up on him and ride on, passing us on the way. When they had gone about as far as we had ridden, they would tie the horse where we would find him. Then they would walk ahead to the next tying place. We called this way of traveling ' riding and tying.'"

How John Adams Traveled

When Patience True's tale is finished, John Adams speaks. He tells us that for more than one hundred years the early Americans traveled chiefly on horseback. He reminds us of the post riders who carried the first letters over the dangerous trails of the forests. We know about them from the trips in which we found out about our mail in another of the Journey Club Travels, *Ourselves and Our City.*

"Little by little these forest paths were widened into roads," John Adams explains. "But the roads were rough and uneven. They were full of ruts and mud puddles. Even after carriages were to be had, many people preferred to ride upon horseback or in sedan chairs carried by Indians or servants. Sedan chairs were

used in England too at about this same time. They were somewhat like the ones we saw with our friend Ah Chee in China. There were also sedan chairs that were slung between two horses. These were the horse-litters in which the fine ladies rode when going on long journeys.

"How you would have laughed at the first carriages in which our forefathers traveled! They had

A post rider delivering a letter

only two wheels, and these were very broad so as not to upset as they slipped and slid over the ruts. The first American carriage of all was called a *chair*. It had two wheels and a seat for two persons with a little perch for the driver out on the shafts.

Sedan chairs were once used in England

The *chaise* that came after was much like the chair, but it had a hood like Taro's jinrikisha and it was more strongly made. Neither had springs. These first carriages were often built by the village blacksmith or wagon-builder. They were rough and crude, and a journey in them was very uncom-fortable.

"I had but little more com-fort when I traveled in the fine stagecoaches of George Wash-

A chaise had two wheels

ington's time. You would have liked their gay colors and the toot-ing horns of the drivers. It was fun to have the people rush to their windows to see us rumble past. These stagecoaches had four huge wheels. The bodies were set high upon their great springs and the passengers had to climb up several steep steps to the doors in their sides. I always liked best to sit with the driver on his high seat up in front.

"The stagecoaches went very fast for those times. There was one that was even called 'the flying machine' because its four horses drew it at such a breath-taking pace. In good weather and with luck I could go from my when our stagecoach upset and the passengers were all spilled out into the mud. The trunks that had been packed on the top of the coach fell off into the road. The men travelers had to get down and help the poor driver

Riding in an early stagecoach

home in Philadelphia to New York in only two days. Perhaps that does not seem fast to the Journey Club members who now go the same distance by train in two hours.

"But often the weather was not good and there were many mishaps. I remember one trip pull his coach out of the mire. Many times coaches were stopped by a poor bridge with gaping holes in its plank floor.

A Night in a Tavern

"When Father and I made our journey to New York we spent the night in a tavern. A great wooden sign hanging over its door pictured a horse painted in red. This sign told us that the name of the inn was the Red Horse Tavern. All stopping places like this were at that time called inns and taverns. No one had ever heard of a hotel.

A stagecoach leaving a tavern

The inn was crowded when we arrived. Father had trouble in finding a bed for himself, and I had to sleep on a pad on the floor. In the morning we were awakened before the sun rose. Our tired horses had been changed for fresh ones and our coach was soon jolting and creaking off again over the muddy roads. We never traveled on Sunday. This was thought to be wrong. Indeed, in some places persons who did so were severely punished.

"My cousin David, who lived in Virginia at this time, used to tell me how glad he was when travelers stopped at his house for the night. Towns were few in Virginia. There were almost no inns. The people were often lonely. They were glad to welcome any traveler and to hear the news he brought with him."

John Adams tells us that even though the roads became better and better, only a few families had private coaches of their own. One had to be rich indeed to afford one. So it was the dream of every one to be able to possess one of these carriages with its galloping steeds. An old schoolbook of those times had this quaint rhyme printed on its cardboard pages:

"He that ne'er learns his A B C
Forever will a blockhead be.
But he that learns these letters fair
Shall have a coach to take the air."

The First American Sleighs

The last part of John Adams' talk tells us of winter travel in Colonial New York and New England. He says the people went about a great deal in huge boys grew hungry, they took out a small hatchet and chopped off a piece of frozen bean porridge. A block of this bean porridge was a part of every pung load. It had been cooked several days before

In winter we ride in a sled called a pung

sleighs and that their favorite winter sport was sleigh-racing. He describes the trip of some New England boys in a box-like sled called a *pung*. With their mother they huddled in the rough body of the sleigh, wrapped to their ears in warm rugs and woolen mufflers. Their father walked in front of the horses. When the and allowed to freeze in a hard chunk. John Adams thinks it may have been this kind of porridge that was meant by the old nursery rhyme:

" Bean porridge hot! Bean porridge cold!
Bean porridge in the pot nine days old!"

CHAPTER 4

A JOURNEY CLUB HIKE

Hurry up, Helen! Come along, Dick! Don't forget your lunch box! The Journey Club is going hiking to-day. We are to have a picnic in the woods several miles out of our town. We could go part of the distance on the street cars or on the train, but the day is so fine we had far rather walk. Laughing and talking, we make our way briskly through the city streets and out over the roads that lead into the country.

"Look at that red bird!" Jack calls out.

"See, there is a starling!" says Mary.

A Journey Club hike

"Let's play a game," Edith cries eagerly. "The one who sees the greatest number of birds, flowers, or other interesting things along the roadside shall be the winner."

We could not play this game so well if we were speeding over the road in an automobile, or if we were riding in a street car or a train. One of the things we enjoy most about walking is that we have time to see the countryside as we pass.

Edith is the winner of our roadside game. She lives in the country and her eyes are keener than ours. She has learned to

We hike along a beautiful stream

keep them wide open and to look about her as she goes from one place to another. Dick tells us an old story of two boys whose names were Good-Eyes and No-Eyes. They had to walk the same distance to their school every day. One morning they were asked to tell what they had seen. No-Eyes said he had not seen anything as he walked along. But Good-Eyes was able to count more than fifty birds and flowers and curious things he had noticed on the same road.

Why We Walk

To-day we are walking for pleasure. We enjoy swinging along the road in our merry group. But often we walk because we must go from one place to the other. We cannot always have automobiles, trains, or trolley cars to take us just where we wish and we must then depend on "Shank's pony," or the "marrow-bone stage," as our legs are sometimes jokingly called. When we visit our neighbors or when we run errands for our mothers, we often find walking the easiest and quickest way to go.

Hiking in the north woods

As we made our world tour to find out about the odd ways of travel in far-away lands, we saw that in Chosen and Africa and other places much of the travel was done on foot. Bob's Uncle Henry once went with a band of explorers through the wild jungles of Africa. There are no roads there. Often the paths are not clear enough for a horse or a donkey.

"My Uncle Henry has often told me of this trip of his," says Bob. "They hired many dark-skinned porters. Some carried their tents, their cooking outfits, and their food. Others bore on their backs the tools, lanterns, and medicines, and the supplies they needed for their weeks in the wilderness. My uncle says that at first they went slowly, for they did not want the porters to give out. They marched only eight miles a day. Later they were able to do fifteen or even twenty miles. Each porter carried about sixty pounds on his back."

Jack has often gone camping with his father in the north woods of our own land. He says that on such trips they load their tents and supplies in a birch-bark canoe like that of Patience True. There are guides to help them. Often they come to the end of a lake or a shallow place in a stream where they have to travel for a time over

Mountain climbers tie themselves together

the land. Then the guides carry the canoes and most of the supplies. Jack and his father also plod along under their share of the load.

In our travels we have seen that in many places men and women balance heavy burdens on top of their heads. They stride swiftly along and seem to have no fear that their bundles will tumble off to the ground. This is because they know how to keep their backs straight and how to hold their heads up. They have carried loads in this way ever since they were children.

Climbing a Snow-capped Mountain

Mary has another story which shows that our legs often take us where nothing else can. She has been reading the tale of a boy who went mountain climbing in the Swiss Alps. She tells us how the mountain climbers go out in bands, and how they tie themselves to each other lest one should slip and be lost in the snowdrifts of the rugged peaks. She says they wear shoes with hob nails in the soles so that they shall not slip and that they dress in their warmest clothes to keep out the cold. Their little packs of food and

Some of our club go wading

supplies are strapped tight to their backs and their arms are left free to grasp their sharp-pointed walking sticks. Each one keeps about twenty feet from his neighbor. They all wear tinted glasses, for the glare of the sun is bad for their eyes.

They first plan their route. Then when they are sure of a good

day they rise with the sun and off they go! Slowly, slowly they travel at first, for they know they must save their strength for later on. A few hours after their start, they stop for a second breakfast. How good it tastes there in the cold air! And, too, it gives them the strength they need to go on with their dangerous climb up the snow-covered slopes and over the glaciers. Now one of them falls! The others stop until he is pulled out of the drifts. They then plod on again. Sometimes they chop steps in the icy walls of a glacier with axes brought for that purpose.

We should think they would find it easier on their way down again. But from Mary's story we learn that it is almost as difficult to come down a mountain as to go up it. It is hard for the mountain climbers to keep themselves from slipping down the icy slopes. When they arrive at their hotel again, their strength is often almost gone.

How to Walk

At last we reach our picnicking spot. We drop down on the grass beneath the shady trees. We have come a long way. We are not so used to long hikes as are the woodland guides or the mountain climbers, and we are glad of a rest. A little brook flows through the woods. Some of us take off our shoes and our stockings and go in wading. The water feels good as it flows about our poor tired feet. When we have rested, we get out our lunch boxes and fall to eating the sandwiches and cake that our mothers have put up for us. What appetites we have! We do not believe that the mountain climbers of Switzerland are more hungry than we. Walking in the fresh air always makes us eager for our next meal.

Bob's brother Tom is a Boy Scout. Bob tells us Tom often goes off on hikes with the rest of his troop. He says the Boy Scouts have strict rules about how they should walk.

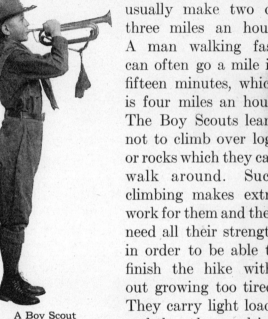

A Boy Scout

"They are careful not to hike too far at one time," says Bob, "and they do not walk fast. Tom says that they usually make two or three miles an hour. A man walking fast can often go a mile in fifteen minutes, which is four miles an hour. The Boy Scouts learn not to climb over logs or rocks which they can walk around. Such climbing makes extra work for them and they need all their strength in order to be able to finish the hike without growing too tired. They carry light loads and they do not drink too much water. One of the troop always has a road map in his pocket so that they may be sure not to lose their way."

As we start home again, Bob shows us the best way for a hiker to carry himself. Look at him as he walks down the road there in front of us! See how straight

Boy Scouts hiking through the woods

they will have to ride home because their feet hurt. They have not worn the right kind of shoes for a long walk like this. Each one has a painful blister on a heel or toe. The rest of us are not at all footsore. We have been careful to put on high shoes with strong soles and low heels. The soldiers in our army take the greatest care of their shoes. They know that they can neither march far nor fight well if their feet are not strongly and comfortably shod.

he stands with his head up, his chest high, and his arms swinging free at his side!

We have now reached the trolley car line that comes out from the city. Two of the girls decide that

CHAPTER 5

OVER ICE AND SNOW

" Jingle Bells !   Jingle Bells !
Jingle all the way.
Oh, what fun it is to ride
In a one-horse open sleigh ! "

Whew ! How cold it is. We snuggle down into the collars of our coats and are glad that we are wearing our sweaters. We pull our woolen gloves well over our wrists. Now and then we swing our arms and slap our chests or run up and down to keep ourselves warm. It is winter. We are standing in the midst of high snowdrifts in front of a farmhouse in Michigan. This farmhouse is the home of Bob's grandmother. She has invited the Journey Club to stop and see her on its trip to the Northlands to find out how people travel to-day over the ice and the snow.

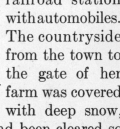

A cutter

Last night when we arrived, Bob's grandmother met us at the railroad station with automobiles. The countryside from the town to the gate of her farm was covered with deep snow, but the road had been cleared so that with skid chains on their wheels, the cars did not get stuck. She tells us that in most snowy parts of the world where the roads are good and where snowplows keep them open, the people may go from one place to another in automobiles even in winter. She says she uses sleighs only when the snow is soft and drifting or too deep to allow her cars to get through. Most of us have never ridden in a sleigh. So we have begged her to let us have a sleigh ride on this cold snowy morning.

"Hark! What are those bells?" Mary cries suddenly.

with their hoofs. Each sleigh has two seats, so wide that three of us can squeeze ourselves into one of them. Warm rugs are tucked in well around our feet. The drivers crack their whips and we are off down the road with a

Sleighing in by-gone days

We stop stamping our numb feet to listen.

"Those are your sleigh bells," Bob's grandmother says smiling. As she speaks the sleighs come round the corner of the farmhouse and draw up before us. The breath of the horses shows white in the frosty air. They toss their heads and paw the snowy road

jingling of the bells that are fastened to the harness of the horses.

How smoothly we ride! Our sleighs glide easily over the snow upon their strong iron runners. The horses' feet make almost no noise. The only sounds are our shouts and the jingle of the sleigh bells. Now and then we

A road in the beautiful snow-capped North

hear other bells. Here comes a one-seated sleigh drawn by a single horse. Bob calls this a cutter. This cutter is beautifully made. Now we are passing a crude sledge that looks like a great box set on low runners. This is a *pung*. It is filled with boxes have already begun. Most of us know how to use ice skates. But we have never seen such skating as this. The shining steel blades of the skates flash in the winter sunshine as the racers dash past. They go at great speed and the crowd cheers the winners.

Through the woods in a pung

and bundles. Heavy loads can be hauled over the snow in sleds like these.

Races on Skates

Bob's grandmother lives near a big city where each year there are held many races over the ice and snow. It is to these races that she is taking us to-day in our dashing sleighs. When we arrive we find that the skating races

Now a man and a girl are dancing on the ice. They whirl and they turn. We clap our hands as they cut circles and figures on the smooth ice with the sharp points of their skates.

Bob's grandmother tells us that the people of the north countries have used skates to go from one place to another for hundreds of years. She thinks that perhaps the very first skater may have tied curved bones on the bottoms of his shoes and pushed himself over the ice with a long staff. She says that in parts of Holland skates are used by every one.

are held on the side of a snow-covered hill. The racers stand upon narrow wooden runners which are tied fast to their feet. How long these runners are!

In Holland children skate to school

Holland is a low country with many swamps. It is often easier to build canals there than to build roads. Holland has a great many such water highways. In the winter the canals are frozen smooth. The children skate back and forth to their schools. Their fathers skate to their work in the mornings, and their mothers glide over the ice as they carry their butter and eggs to the market.

Look at that man carrying his skis upright in his hand! Each ski is three or four inches wide, and it is longer than he is tall. Bob says that some skis are almost ten feet long. He has seen skiing

Skis are long flat runners

contests before on his other visits to his grandmother, so he explains them to us.

"That hillside over there is the route of the ski-jumpers," he says. "That raised place half way down the path has been

Ski-Jumping

The races we like best to-day are the ski (skee) races. These

A runway for skiing

carefully built up and well covered with snow. You will see why in a minute."

A ski-jumper is just starting. With arms outstretched he slides down the steep hill-path. Faster and faster he comes! See, he has now reached the snowy mound at the half-way point. Look! Look! He leaps high above the snowy slide. We hold our breaths as he seems fairly to fly through the air. What a jump he makes!

At last he drops down again to the path and rushes on to the bottom of the hill. The jumper who leaps farthest will win the prize in this contest. The longest ski-jump that we know of covered nearly two hundred and fifty feet.

Skis first came from Norway. There every one knows how to tramp upon skis and the Norwegian children learn to use them almost as soon as they begin to walk. In the cold winters both there and in Sweden the farmers and soldiers go for great distances over the snow on wooden runners like these. They travel fast on their skis.

As our sleighs take us back to the farm, Mary asks us if we remember our tramp on broad snowshoes in our Journey Club trip to find out about furs, and Helen tells us of tobogganing at a winter resort. Dick describes some races between sailboats with iron runners fastened under them. He says such ice boats can skim over the frozen lakes as fast as an express train, some of them going a mile in a minute.

Norwegian children on skis

In the Far-North

It is a long journey from the Michigan farmhouse to our next stopping place. We have heard about the reindeer of the Land of the Snows ever since the first Christmas we can remember. We have all read of Dasher and Dancer, Prancer and Vixen, of Comet and Cupid and Donder and Blitzen, the eight tiny reindeer in the poem about Santa Claus. So we are eager to see how real reindeer are driven hitched to real sleds. At first some of the Journey Club members thought we should go to Lapland, the earliest home of the reindeer. But when we found out that in Alaska, a part of our own United States, there are also many reindeer, we decided to choose that place instead.

The rivers and lakes of Alaska are all frozen solid in winter and there are but few railroads. So we have flown here in airplanes that brought us to Seattle and then on and on to that far part of the Northland where most of our

Tobogganing in Canada

Eskimos live. We have some old friends here. They are Ikwa and Too-Kee, the Eskimo boy and girl whom we have met on our other travels.

We had thought it cold in Michigan. Here, so much nearer the North Pole, it is far colder. We shiver and our teeth chatter as we trudge through the snow

to Ikwa's home. He offers to sell us some fine fur trousers and coats. He calls the coats *parkas*. How funny we look in them! They have huge furry hoods that we pull over our heads. Only our eyes and our noses are to be seen.

Ikwa calls to his father and tells him we have come all the way from the United States to see his reindeer. Ikwa's father is well-to-do. He has a large herd of reindeer.

Eskimo girls wearing parkas

Now Ikwa is leading out a beautiful deer. The reindeer is much smaller than we had thought. He is not much bigger than a good-sized pony. He is about four feet high and so tame that we can safely stroke his chocolate-brown back. Underneath his body, the fur is almost white. Some of the reindeer in this herd are spotted and one or two are all white.

What great branching horns the reindeer has! Ikwa tells us he sheds them every year and grows an entirely new set. His horns push the leaves and twigs away from his eyes as he goes through the tangled woods in the summer. Reindeer fight with their horns. Sometimes a battle between two deer has to be stopped lest one of them should be killed.

We Ride behind Reindeer

Ikwa's father is putting a collar around the neck of the reindeer. He fastens a wide band about the animal's body. A long strap is tied to the base of his horns and is passed underneath his chest and between his legs. It is with this strap that Ikwa's father drives his reindeer.

Reindeer are about as big as ponies

When the low wooden sled is hitched to the reindeer, we take turns in riding for short distances over the snow. The reindeer travels swiftly, but he is not very strong and cannot be driven for many days at a time. He can make a speed of ten miles an hour, and he will draw his sled with a small load for thirty or forty miles in a day. The sled is light. It is made of pieces of driftwood held together with strips of hide instead of nails.

"What does he eat?" Edith asks Too-Kee. She knows how

Reindeer pull sleds

important food is for the horses that work on her father's farm.

"We do not have to feed him, for he finds his own food," Too-Kee replies. "His name comes from the Lapp word *reino* meaning 'to pasture.' He is the 'animal that pastures himself.' In summer our reindeer eat wild grasses, moss, and weeds, and in winter they paw their way down to their favorite gray moss that grows underneath the snow. The reindeer lives on this moss. He does not need shelter even in the iciest weather. The colder it is the better he likes it."

Ikwa tells us the parkas we are

wearing are made of reindeer skins. He says reindeer milk is good and reindeer meat is delicious. Indeed, the reindeer is the Eskimo's best friend. The reindeer is the Eskimo's cow, his ox, his horse, and his sheep. The reindeer gives him food and clothing, and draws his loads for him for miles over the snowy wilderness. The reindeer has been called "the camel of the frozen desert" because he is so well fitted to travel through the soft snow drifts. His hoof is wide. It is hollowed out underneath so that when he sets his foot down, the hoof spreads and does not sink so easily into the snow.

In winter reindeer eat the moss beneath the snow

The first reindeer were brought into Alaska from Norway and Siberia. Now there are more than three hundred and fifty thousand of these sturdy animals here. About one-third of the herds are owned by Americans like ourselves, who live in this Northland. Many of their deer are killed each year for their meat and shipped to the markets of the United States.

Sleds Drawn by Dogs

As our planes rise again into the air, we shout our thanks and good-byes to our Eskimo friends. We are now off for Nome, one of the most important little cities of this Northland of ours. There we are to see how dogs do the same work that these reindeer do for the Eskimos and that our horses and automobiles do for us at home.

An Alaskan boy named Ted is to be our guide while we are in Nome. His father has several teams of sled dogs, and Ted himself knows how to harness them and how to drive them over the snowy trails. He invites us to ride into the country on his dog sleds. We go with him to hitch up the dogs. Many of them are

lying curled up on the snow. They look like furry balls with their noses tucked so snugly under their tails.

"Here, Rover! Here, Blizzard! Come, Leo and Bubbles. Ginger! Arrow! Here, Ring!" At Ted's calls the dogs jump to their feet and swarm about us. Ted says they are of two kinds. Some are

Each dog team has a leader

huskies and some *malamutes*. He thinks some of these dogs are part wolf. They look like wolves with their great gray bodies and their long pointed noses. Their coats are heavier than those of the dogs in our warmer climate back home.

Now Ted brings out the dog sleds. They are long and low with rails along their sides to hold the loads on. They are put together with ropes made of hide

Bobsleds drawn by horses are used where roads are good

instead of with nails, and have strips of iron fastened on their runners. It does not take Ted long to harness the dogs. They have been carefully trained and all know their places. There are seven dogs in each team and each team has a lead dog who runs in front. He sets the pace. Now and then he looks around to see that all the dogs of his team are doing their share. If he finds one that is lazy, he gives him a sharp nip on the ear or the leg.

Ted and his brothers trot behind us. They guide us by means of the two handles on the backs of the sleds. Now and then Ted cracks his long whip, and calls out sharply, "Mush! Mush!"

"Is Mush our lead dog's name?" Mary asks. Ted laughs heartily. "No," he explains, "Mush means 'Go faster.' It comes from 'March' (Marche) the call of the early French dog-drivers in Canada. I drive the dogs mostly with my voice. 'Gee' means 'To the right,' 'Haw' means 'To the left,' and 'Whoa' means 'Stop.'"

We ride swiftly out of the town over the snow-covered road. Now and again we pass a bobsled drawn by teams of horses. This trail is good enough and wide enough for horse-drawn sleighs.

But soon we leave the wide trail and take one of the smaller ones. Dog-sleds can go many places where horses cannot. These sled dogs are strong. A good team will draw a heavy load over the snow sixty miles in one day. It can keep up the pace for many days. For long winter journeys in Alaska dogs are often far better than either reindeer or horses.

A gold miner's dog

fish and rice. They have to be tied to stakes far enough apart to prevent them from fighting over their food. They eat only one meal a day and that is always after their day's work is done. When their stomachs are full, they lie down on the snow and bite the icicles out of their toes, lest their feet should grow sore.

We are wrapped up in rugs as we sit on our sleds, but it is so cold here that we are glad of our parkas which we bought from the Eskimos. The temperature is many degrees below zero. Our noses are red and our cheeks are like ice when we return from our ride. We stop to help Ted give the dogs their daily meal of dried

Ted tells us that many of the mail carriers in Alaska use dog-sleds in winter. In the summer these dog-horses are sometimes hitched to little cars that run upon rails out to the mining camps. Ted calls this means of travel a "pup-mobile." In going down hill, the dogs are unharnessed. They jump on the car and ride until the next hill is reached.

CHAPTER 6

OUR FRIEND, THE HORSE

"This is Dobbin," says Edith. She takes a lump of sugar from her pocket and lets the big brown horse eat it off the palm of her hand. The Journey Club is meeting on her father's farm which is out in the country not far from our town. We have come into the barn to see the horses and mules that work on her farm, for to-day we wish to find out how these animals help us to travel and to carry our loads.

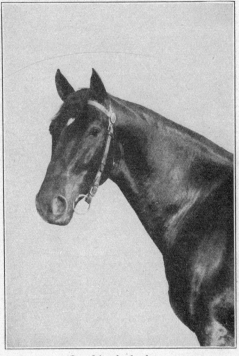

Our friend, the horse

"Dobbin is old," Edith explains. "For nearly twenty years he has been the faithful servant of my family. He has carried us all for many a mile, and he knows how to do all kinds of farm work. He is the wisest horse in our stable." Dobbin seems to know that Edith is talking about him, for he rubs her shoulder gently with his soft velvety nose.

"Why don't we ask him to talk to us about horses," Jack says, jokingly. "Come, Dobbin, tell us about your ancestors and what you horses do to help us to travel."

We all wish that clever old Dobbin really could talk. If he gave it to his children to play with. They may have made it into a pet. When it grew up, they may have found out how big and strong their horse was,

Horses drew war chariots in ancient times

only could, the story we should hear would go something like this.

Dobbin's Forefathers

"The people of savage times did not know at first what we horses could do to help them. So they used to hunt us and kill us for food. I suppose that one day some hunter caught a little lost colt, and taking pity upon it, did not kill it at once. Perhaps how easy to ride, and how useful in carrying their burdens from one place to the other. Ever since that time we horses have been the faithful friend and servant of man. We have carried him and his loads in peace and in war for thousands of years.

"In the old days in Egypt and in Greece we were used chiefly to pull the chariots of war over the military roads. From that day to this we have carried men of all the armies of the world into the thick of the battle. There is an old verse that shows how

"For hundreds of years we horses were used mostly for riding and working. We plowed the fields. We drew the clumsy

Horses plow many of our fields

important we horses are in times of war. It goes like this:

" ' For want of a nail, the shoe was lost,
For want of the shoe, the horse was lost,
For want of the horse, the rider was lost,
For want of the rider, the battle was lost,
For want of the battle, the kingdom was lost,
And all for the want of a horseshoe nail.'

work-carts. Later when men learned how to make the first carriages, we pulled them through the mud and the mire of the early roads."

What We Owe to Horses

"You have no doubt heard of the part we horses played in the making of your country. We carried the mails over the forest trails. We drew stagecoaches from one settlement to the other. It was we horses, together with oxen and mules, that plodded into the wildernesses of the West with the pioneers in their covered wagons and their heavily-loaded pack trains. We stood by them in their fights with the Indian the automobile. The automobile goes much faster than a horse and so of course people prefer it. Bob says his father's automobile can do as much work as thirty or forty horses, pulling together. It is not strange that this new and more rapid way of travel is

Stagecoaches were drawn by horses

raiders, and we helped them to turn the soil of the wild plains into fertile farms. Without the aid of horses they could not have built the wonderful cities and towns in which you live to-day.''

Parts of Dobbin's story would tell us of the carriages in which our grandmothers rode. I am afraid we might see tears in his eyes when he talked of his enemy, fast driving the horse from the streets of our cities. We have often heard our fathers and mothers talk of buggies and dog-carts, of victorias and landaus and hansom cabs. But many of us have never seen any one riding for pleasure in a horse-drawn vehicle.

"We may not be wanted now to draw carriages,'' Dobbin's

story would go on, "but the farmers cannot get along without us. Machines and gasoline

A draft horse

be used. There, we horses are needed as badly as ever. Farm horses like me are called draft horses. We are heavier and larger than those that were formerly hitched to fine carriages, or the thoroughbreds raised for riding and racing. There are still about fifteen million of us left on the farms. Alas, we horses do not bring high prices to-day, and as more and more of these automobiles are built, we shall be less and less wanted."

Dobbin should tell us also about his cousin, the mule. This sturdy animal is much prized for farm work. He eats less than a horse and he is especially strong. His father was a donkey and his mother a horse. He has his father's long ears and scrubby tail, and also his loud bray, "eee-aaw," "eee-aaw." But he is larger than his father, getting his size from his mother's side of the family. Mules are widely used for hauling heavy gun car-

tractors may take our place for much of their farm work, but there are still many parts of the country where these cannot easily

Dobbin's cousins, the mules

not to let his horses drink too much water or to eat when they are hot and tired. They are brushed and combed every day so that their coats fairly shine.

How airy this barn is! And how clean the stalls in which the horses are standing! Edith tells us a clean stable is important in keeping a horse healthy and strong.

riages and for other rough work in our army camps.

We Explore the Barn

Edith takes us over the barn to show us the bins and the lofts where the horses' food is stored. She says the grass of the fields forms a part of their summer feed, but in winter they must eat in their stalls. We jump about in the hay in the loft under the roof and run our hands down into the bins filled with oats and corn. Edith says a horse's stomach is not large. He must be given small meals several times in one day. Her father is careful

Edith is fond of horses. She says they know a great deal. Some of the ones we are looking at have to have special locks on

Dobbin's stall is clean

the doors of their stalls, for they know how to lift the latch with their teeth. A good horse will find his way home over the darkest road when even the

Paul Revere's ride

driver cannot see how to go. Dick asks us if we have ever noticed the horses of milk delivery wagons. They seem to know the stops as well as their drivers. They halt of their own accord and wait until the bottles have been left on the door-

step. Then they go on to the next house.

There are many famous horses in history. A poem we like is about the midnight ride of Paul Revere. One stanza of this poem, which was written by Longfellow, is

" A hurry of hoofs in a village
    street,
A shape in the moonlight,
    a bulk in the dark,
And beneath, from the peb-
    bles, in passing, a spark
Struck out by a steed flying
    fearless and fleet.''

Carriages for Our Museum

After our day with Edith on the farm, we make a search for pictures and models of carts, coaches, and carriages drawn by horses to put into our Museum. Bob himself has made a model of an old Roman chariot. Its rough low wheels are held in place with wooden pins thrust through the ends of the axle. The chariot is a little platform on wheels, closed in the front and open in the back. Chariots had no seats and the drivers stood as they urged their steeds over the rough Roman roads.

Mary has brought a picture of an early settler's cart. It looks like a box set on an axle with two round disks for wheels. The wheels were rude slices of the trunk of a huge tree. They were clumsy and heavy. Later, pieces were cut out of them to make them lighter, and finally wheels with spokes were invented. Such wheels were much lighter and stronger. There was an iron strip around the rim to keep it from wearing out. Mary says that in those early days an ox and a horse were often hitched up together.

"My pictures show the four-wheeled coaches and stagecoaches

A stagecoach of Queen Elizabeth's day

An early colonial wagon

A phaeton

of George Washington's time," says Dick. "George Washington loved horses. He had a great many in his stables at Mt. Vernon, and he took the best care of them. Do you remember we saw his old coach on our Journey Club trip to Washington last spring? See, this picture shows the leather straps upon which the body of the coach swung. They held it off the stiff axles and were supposed to make it ride easily. But the coach jerked and jolted and the body swung this way and that. When these straps were first used, the coaches were called 'trembling carriages.'" It was not until later when iron and steel springs were invented that they were at all comfortable to ride in."

Dick tells us also that men often did not choose to ride in these first coaches. They thought they

An omnibus

were only for women and children who were not strong enough to go upon horseback.

Next to our pictures of coaches, we place a drawing of a chaise, and Helen prints neatly on a card the verses of Oliver Wendell Holmes about the "One-Hoss Shay," as such a carriage was often nicknamed. This poem tells of the Deacon's wonderful "shay" that lasted exactly one hundred years before it was shaken to pieces by an earthquake.

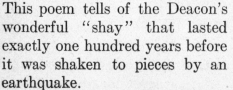

A brougham

A Covered Wagon

The most interesting of all this exhibit is a model of a covered wagon with its team of six horses. It was lumbering vehicles like this that carried the first bands of travelers westward across the United States. Such wagons were often called "prairie schooners" because they were shaped like a ship upon wheels. The bottoms of their bodies were curved like broad canoes. They were built up high both in front and in back to keep the freight from slipping and sliding as the wagons went up and down the steep mountain trails.

Covered wagons like these were first built in Pennsylvania. For a long while they were called Conestoga wagons, because this region was the land of the Conestoga Indians, and the town where they were made was named Conestoga. Whole families lived in them during their journeyings over the western plains. They had under their canvas roofs beds and stoves and tables and chairs. When the weather was too bad to allow the travelers to camp out of doors on the ground, they ate and slept and horses, wound their slow painful trails over the hills and the mountains, the plains and the

A covered wagon, or Conestoga wagon

in their wagons. Conestoga wagons were really houses on wheels.

Jack has found out that many of these first American travelers banded together and kept their covered wagons close to each other so that if the Indians came they could better drive them away. Thousands of such wagon trains, drawn by oxen prairies, bearing the brave men and women who opened up our great country for us. Until railroads were laid many years later, they formed the only means of travel inland from the sea coast. Think of the difference between their months of hardship, and the five or six days of comfortable travel that we

Horses draw our milk wagons

make in going from one coast of our country to the other!

The Carriages of Our Grandmothers

From some old magazines which Helen found in her attic, we cut much in country towns. The most elegant of all is the victoria in which the fine ladies and gentlemen rode behind their teams of high-stepping horses. Lastly there are pictures of the horse

Horses and mules help to fill our silos

pictures of the carriages that were being used when the automobile came. These were comfortable-looking with their graceful bodies and their neat rubber-tired wheels. Here is a buggy with its four light wheels and its seat just right for two. And this is a station wagon of the kind used so cabs and hansoms that served as the taxis of the past, and the omnibus that carried many people at one time.

As we arrange our exhibit on the shelves of our Museum, it seems strange to us that these carriages that thronged the streets of our cities so short a time ago

Horses draw our hay wagons

should have all disappeared. Here and there in the country we might find some of them still used, but with the coming of the good but not very expensive automobile, they have been largely put aside even there.

Edith's gift to the Museum is a collection of snapshots taken on her father's farm. They show Dobbin and the other farm horses at work, hitched to the plow, the cultivator, and the harrow, the farm wagon, the mower, the binder, the hay rack, and the other farm machines. She has put in also a snapshot of a span of oxen and a mule-team and of her pony, Brown Beauty.

Brown Beauty

CHAPTER 7

A LETTER ABOUT BICYCLES

"I have a letter to read to the Journey Club to-day," says our president, Mary, as she opens our meeting. "I found it up in our attic when I was going through an old trunk hunting for pictures of carriages for our Journey Club Museum. It was written by my father when he was a boy no older than I. It tells all about bicycles."

Every member of our club has a bicycle. We often ride to school upon them and to-day we have brought them with us to the Journey Club meeting. We have decided that we shall next find out about these bicycles of ours and how they help us to go from one place to another. We think it will be interesting to hear from this boy bicycle-owner of so long ago. His letter reads:

Mary reads a letter

Dear Cousin Ann:

I am sorry that you were sick in bed on Christmas and I hope that you are sitting up by now. Perhaps you will enjoy hearing what a good time we had at our house. We had a big family dinner and such a lot of presents around the Christmas tree. The best one of all I got was — you never would guess what. A bicycle! I have been hoping for a bicycle for more than a year, but I was afraid that my father would think me too young to be trusted

A woman's bicycle

out on the streets with all those speeding horses and carriages. But he didn't! There under the tree I found my beautiful *Rover*, shining with its glossy black paint and its nickel trimmings and with a real bell fixed on its handlebars.

Usually I like lots of snow for Christmas. But this year I was only too glad there was none so that I could go right out and learn to ride my bicycle. Aunt Bess learned to ride her "wheel" at a bicycle riding school.

An expert cyclist taught her how to sit properly and how to manage the handlebars and the pedals.

My big brother, John, taught me. He took hold of the little saddle and pushed me along. He held me straight until I learned to balance myself. I fell only once. That was when I was going down a small hill. Then I lost my balance and off I went, head over heels into a ditch. John laughed when he saw that I was not hurt. He said it was as pretty a "header" as he had ever seen. I have practiced every day since and I never take "headers" now. I have

A "header" from a velocipede

learned to coast down hill with my feet off the pedals.

Everybody is riding a bicycle here in our city. Men and women, and girls and boys are on black costumes that fitted like tights. The handlebars of the racing bicycles are curved down like a ram's horn, and the racers bend almost double as they ride.

A bicycle race of the past

all crazy about them. They ride them to business and they use them for pleasure. Our doctor thinks bicycling is one of the very best kinds of exercise. John says there are bicycle clubs all over the United States. He has told me about a race from Chicago to Pullman, Illinois, in which there were a thousand bicyclers. Most of these racers had

Women's bicycles of early days

They go very fast. When we speed on our bicycles, we call it "scorching."

Some women bicyclers wear a kind of full trousers called bloomers, and yesterday I saw a man and a girl riding tandem. Their wheel had two seats and two sets of pedals and two handlebars. The girl sat in front with the man behind. His seat was a

A school for learning to ride the "dandy horse"

little higher so that he could see over her head. As they went by, some children standing near me began to sing part of the new song "Daisy Bell":

"You'll look sweet
Upon the seat
Of a bicycle built for two."

Father has a book about bicycles. It has many pictures in it. I found one machine that was called the "Father of the Bicycle." It was not at all like mine. It had two wheels fastened at each end of a long bar of wood. There were no pedals. The rider sat on the wooden perch and made the machine go by touching the ground with his feet. He really ran along as he sat. He steered with a straight little handlebar of wood.

This odd machine was invented more than one hundred years ago by Baron von Drais, a forester on a huge estate. With it he could make the rounds of the forest paths more quickly than he could walk. His machine was called a *draisine.* When it was first used in England it was nicknamed a "dandy horse," a "hobby horse," and a "swift walker."

A few people were pleased with the dandy horse. But it did not become really popular until some one decided to add pedals, making the velocipede, as the first wheels were called. English bicycles of those times were often dubbed "bone-shakers."

How you would laugh if you could see the picture I found of my father sitting on one of those old-fashioned velocipedes! He is perched high in the air, on a tiny saddle that is built above a wheel higher than your head. There is another tiny wheel behind this to help the rider to balance himself on the high one. Sometimes the little balance wheel was placed in the front instead. Father tells me it was hard to climb up on the seat of his velocipede. He often fell off. The velocipede was really dangerous and many riders were hurt.

It was to make bicycling safe that the bicycle-makers thought of having both wheels low and of the same size. That is why they called the first bicycles like mine "safeties." Each year the bicycle-makers have built them better and better. They have given them air-filled rubber tires

A velocipede

instead of tires of hard rubber. These make them ride easily. They have put ball-bearings in the wheels and they have arranged the handlebars so that they can be lowered or raised to suit each rider. They have also made their leather saddles comfortable to sit upon.

My bicycle has a coaster-brake. With this I can stop my wheel quickly by pressing back on the pedals. The coaster-brake is splendid to use going down hill. When I coast without it, I go almost too fast. I feel just like a bird. In father's book on bicycles there is this verse about coasting:

" With lifted feet, hands still,
  I am poised and down the hill
  Dart with gleeful mind.
  The air goes by in a wind,
  Swifter and yet more swift,
  Till the heart with a mighty lift,
  Makes the lungs laugh, the throat cry,
  Oh, bird, see! See, bird, I fly!"
  — HENRY CHARLES BEECHING

Father likes to go bicycling with me. He belongs to the League of American Wheelmen. That League is helping to get better roads built so that we shall soon be able to ride more comfortably. He says there are more than three hundred bicycle factories in the United States and that they make over a million wheels a year. Father's bicycle was expensive. It cost about one hundred and fifty dollars, and it weighs nearly fifty pounds.

I want to thank you for the beautiful knit cap you sent me for Christmas. It is just what I need to wear when I am on my wheel, for it does not blow off. John is calling me now to go for a ride. I hope you will soon get well so that I can show you how to ride my bicycle too. Good-by.

Your cousin,
Henry

Our Bicycles To-day

"Put on your hats and sweaters and get your bicycles out," says Mary. "The next part of our meeting to-day is to be held down town in Mr. Sterling's bicycle store. He has invited the

Some of our club on bicycles

Journey Club to come and look at the latest bicycle models."

Now we are off. We keep well to the right side of the street so as to be out of the way of any automobiles. The warm sun is shining and the breeze blows in our faces. As we pedal along, we think bicycling is one of the very nicest ways to travel.

In Mr. Sterling's shop we find many new bicycles. They are painted in bright colors, red, blue,

Bicycles are used by messenger boys

brown, and green. Their handle-bars and trimmings shine like silver. There are special bicycles for girls without the crossbar between the wheels which boys' bicycles have. Mr. Sterling is interested in hearing about the letter Mary has just read us.

"Before the boy that wrote that letter had grown into a young man the bicycle was no

longer so popular," he says. "You see, the automobile was invented a few years later. The automobile was so much more comfortable and could go so much faster that people gradu-ally gave up their cycling for automobiling. Now each year in all the bicycle fac-tories of the United States there are made only about one-fourth of the million that were turned out in the days when Mary's letter was written. Mes-sengers and men in cer-tain kinds of work use bicycles for their daily duties. Boys and girls like you ride them for the fun of it. But I will wager that none of you has ever seen a grown man or woman riding a bicycle purely for pleasure."

"I have," says Bob. "When we were traveling in Europe, we saw young men and women riding their bicycles in groups along the sides of the roads."

"Ah, yes, in Europe," Mr. Ster-ling replies, smiling. "There, many people are too poor to afford automobiles. So they buy bicycles instead. And the young people seem to enjoy their bicycle rides as much as we do our drives in fast automobiles. A favorite sport of the French is bicycle

A French girl delivering bread on a bicycle

racing. Not long ago a contest was held to choose the most popular athlete of all France. The winner was a famous bicycle rider."

Mr. Sterling tells us that the latest bicycles are only about half as heavy as the one Mary's father rode. He says they cost one-fourth or one-fifth as much as

did those first "safeties." He warns us to be very careful when we ride along the busy streets of our cities. Where the traffic is thick and there are many automobiles, bicycling is dangerous.

Motor Cycles

The greater part of Mr. Sterling's store is given up to motor cycles. He says that the motor cycle is really just a heavy bicycle with a gasoline motor to turn its wheels. The success of the motor cycle is another reason why so few bicycles are sold now.

"A motor cycle will go as fast as an automobile," says Mr. Sterling. "One gallon of gasoline will carry it fifty miles and more, so you see it is not costly to run. Then, too, the legs of its rider do not grow tired from constant pedaling, for the motor cycle runs by its own power."

Mr. Sterling shows us the little tank for gasoline that makes the motor go. There is another tank for oil. He says that the plan of the engine of a motor cycle is much the same as that of a four-wheeled automobile.

In the World War motor cycles were used to carry messages from

Policemen use fast motor cycles

one part of the battle grounds to another. Our police find them useful in controlling the traffic on our streets and our highroads. Motor cycles are small. They are easy to store away. But they are not so cheap as a bicycle. Some cost almost as much as a small automobile.

Mr. Sterling thinks motor cycles are specially good for long journeys when one has not much baggage. He says motor cyclists on such trips should be covered from head to foot to protect themselves from the mud and the dust. They often wear great goggles that shield their eyes from bits of flying dirt. Motor cyclists are not so well sheltered as travelers in an automobile. Bicycles and motor cycles are not pleasant for journeys on rainy days.

"Here is a side car." Bob calls us to come and look at a motor cycle which has a cradle-shaped car built out on one side. This little car is supported by another wheel on the outside. We see

A motor cycle side car

that the car is of metal and that it is fastened to the motor cycle by bars of steel. By means of its side car the motor cycle can carry an extra passenger, and a small amount of baggage can be packed away in its body. When it is not wanted, the side car can be easily taken off and the motor cycle used alone.

CHAPTER 8

THE IRON HORSE

"Did you ever see so many people?" cries Helen as we make our way through the crowds that are getting off the train with us. We have come all the way from our own city to a town not far from Baltimore to see the wonderful "Fair of the Iron Horse." As soon as we read in the newspapers of this exhibition that was to be held by the oldest

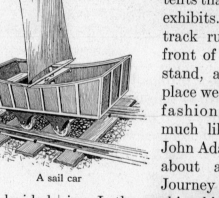

A sail car

railroad in our country, we decided that we must see it. So here we are! And with us there are thousands and thousands of other people, men and women, and boys and girls, all interested in finding out the story of the railroads and how they help us in our everyday life.

Our seats are good. They are in the first row of the vast grandstand. Spread out before us are the fair grounds with low buildings and tents that house the exhibits. A railroad track runs just in front of the grandstand, and at one place we see an old-fashioned tavern much like the one John Adams told us about at another Journey Club meeting. In the sunshine, high above us, there float the flags of the United States and of the railroad whose birthday this parade is to celebrate.

Travel in the Days before the Railroad

"Ladies and Gentlemen!" A deep voice booms out above our

heads. Dick is the first to see the owner of the voice. He is standing out in the center of the parade ground and talking into a little round metal disk such as radio speakers use. His voice whoops fill the air and a dozen real Indians gallop by on their horses. We enjoy this first part of the parade, for we have ourselves found out about many of these early ways of getting about.

At the Fair of the Iron Horse

comes to our ears through several huge horns above us up under the roof. It sounds as loud as if he were standing beside us.

"Ladies and Gentlemen," the voice begins. "The first part of the parade will show you how people traveled before there were railroads." As he speaks, wild

The drag cart, the birch-bark canoe, and riders on horseback are already shown by pictures and models in our Journey Club Museum.

We are interested, too, in the canal boat with its quaintly dressed passengers and its cargo of boxes and bales. Perhaps the finest of all the first part of the pageant is the George Washington Coach, with its prancing horses. It is much like our own pictures of Colonial coaches. It has coachmen and footmen in livery and two outriders in white

"Nearly three hundred years ago," says the deep voice over our heads, "there were several railroads in England. But they were not much like our railroads to-day. They had rough wooden rails fastened to crossties, and

Float showing founders of our first railroad

wigs, scarlet suits, and three-cornered hats.

The First Railroads

Look at the float that comes next! It is made like a brick house with part of the walls taken out so we can see in. Who are the men sitting in those old-fashioned chairs? Listen! Perhaps the voice from the horns will tell us something about them.

their cars were drawn by horses. They were built for short distances only and were used to bring coal out of the mines. The very first railways in America were much like these English roads. One, three miles long, was laid from a granite quarry near Quincy, Massachusetts. Over its wooden rails, horses drew little cars filled with stone blocks for the monument on Bunker Hill.

"The men you see sitting at this table lived about one hundred years ago. They are here planning the first real railroad in America. It ran from Baltimore to Ellicott City, in Maryland. They are probably discussing some wonderful steam engines which had lately been made in England and France. One of them tells the old story of James Watt, the Scotch boy who found out what steam could do by watching it lift the lid of his mother's teakettle. These men have letters from friends in France and in England that describe wonderful steam carriages that run over the roads without any horses. These letters say steam engines can be made to pull cars of coal over wooden rails at a speed of fifteen miles an hour. They all laugh when one man calls this 'traveling by teakettle.' They are sure that some kind of railway is needed here in America, but they are not at all sure that this strange steam engine will work well or safely enough for the railway they plan to have. They think it best to have their own cars drawn by horses at first."

The next part of the parade shows us some of the different ways in which cars were pulled over the rails of our first railroads. Here is a horse car. It looks like a little cabin on wheels. Leaning from its windows are ladies dressed in quaint gowns and tiny bonnets. We laugh at one man with long whiskers and a bright red vest who runs to catch up with the car. He has no difficulty in doing so, the horse moves so slowly.

An early passenger train

Jamie Watt watching the teakettle

passing now? It is a sail car. The wind was supposed to blow it along over the rails. Sail cars often had accidents, too. Once a strong wind blew away a mast and its sail, and with them several unlucky passengers.

"Traveling by Teakettle"

"The new railroad was built," the story of the parade goes on, "and within a short time horses were pulling over its rails crude horse cars like the one you have just seen. Strips of iron had been placed over the wooden rails to make them stronger, and every one was delighted with this wonderful new

Next comes a treadmill car. The weight of a horse walking up an endless platform turns its wheels and makes it go. Our speaker tells us that this car was tried out for a short time. But one day it ran into a cow and was turned over into a ditch. After that accident the treadmill car was given up.

What is this queer car

Float showing a treadmill car

means of travel. But the four-legged engines were not used long. Letters kept coming across the ocean telling of the success of steam engines that had been built by a man named George Stephenson. He had improved his iron horses more and more until at last they were being used instead of real horses on several of the British railroads.

motives have, except that, of course, its parts were small and crude. The *Rocket* went at what was then thought a dangerous speed — about fourteen miles an hour.

"The first steam engine to run on an American railroad was built in England," says the parade story-teller. "It had a fierce British lion painted on its side

Tom Thumb races the horse car

There were twenty-eight railways in England when our first American roads were laid down. They were almost all for hauling coal, and they carried but few passengers. The very first steam engines did not run smoothly, and horses still had a place between the rails.

"Stephenson's engine, the *Rocket*, was the first important locomotive. It was the father of the huge puffing giants we ride behind to-day. It had about the same parts that our great loco-

and it was called the *Stourbridge Lion*. Many of our early railroads used locomotives from England. But the American engineers soon fell to work to build engines themselves, and in 1830 a man named Peter Cooper brought forth the tiny locomotive, *Tom Thumb*.

"At first the people of Maryland did not believe in these iron horses. They thought four-legged horses were far more dependable. One day a race was held between a gray horse and the puffing *Tom Thumb* engine of Peter Cooper. When the race showed that the engine could travel faster than the horse, *Tom Thumb* was regarded with more respect, and it was proved that Americans could make iron horses that would go."

eral men and women in old-fashioned costumes ride in the rude cabin behind it.

An Old-fashioned Train

Next there puffs past us one of the very first passenger trains of our country. It is drawn by an

An old-fashioned train

"Here comes *Tom Thumb* now," Bob cries out, as a funny little engine puffs noisily past us. It looks like a huge iron bottle out for an airing on a four-wheeled truck. This is a model of that first tiny locomotive. A man dressed to represent Peter Cooper stands upon the truck, a wrench in his hand for use in case the engine should break down. Sev-

engine named the *De Witt Clinton*, one of the earliest built in America. Between it and the coaches there is a little truck upon which we see barrels filled with logs of wood. This is the fuel with which the boiler's fire is made. The *De Witt Clinton* pulls three quaint coaches painted in bright colors. Fifteen passengers are riding inside each coach and upon the seats on its roof. The coaches look just like the old horse-drawn road coaches of George Washington's time.

At first we think we should like to ride in the seats on the tops of the coaches. But we soon change our minds when we see how the smoke and the cinders from the puffing engine are blowing back

The Tiger

into the faces of the passengers who sit there. Look, there is one woman putting up her umbrella to keep the cinders out of her eyes.

This train goes much faster than the little *Tom Thumb*. The *De Witt Clinton* and another engine called the *Best Friend* were the first two large locomotives to be used here. We see that the coaches are hitched together by chains about three feet long. Now the train is stopping. What a bump! The passengers are almost thrown out of their seats. We think such cars must have been very uncomfortable. Trains

like these did not run at night, for they did not have headlights and it was thought too dangerous. When it rained the engine was often left behind and horses used instead.

There are several of these early trains in the parade. Their engines are manned by men with long beards who wear shirts of red flannel. Their freight is carried at the back in barrels and boxes. The railroads in those days often owned only the tracks and the engines. Factories and persons who wanted to ship goods had their own cars. They paid the railroads to haul these cars over the rails from one town to another.

As the parade passes, we see how engines were gradually made bigger and better. Our story-teller says that the wooden rails, strapped with iron, were soon changed for rails of cast iron and then of steel. He says that as soon as it was found that railroads were a success, more and more were laid down over our land. The covered wagons of the pioneers pushed their way into the wilderness of our West, and railroads followed them. Our government helped the private railroad builders by giving them lands and by having maps and surveys made for them.

All these early roads were built at great risk to the brave men who laid their rails across the hills and the valleys of our unknown

A Talk with an Engineer

The last ones of the procession of engines are now gliding past us. These are the modern giant locomotives that pull our trains over the plains and the mountains at such a great speed.   Some weigh

Rails of shiny steel carry our trains

country with its Indians and wild beasts. We should remember what we owe them as we ride over the shining tracks that now cover our land from north to south and from east to west. The United States to-day has more than six times as many miles of railroad tracks as any other country upon earth.

several hundred thousand pounds. They are strong enough to pull a train of loaded cars a mile long. There are steam giants here from most of the railroads of the United States and some that have been sent from Great Britain and Canada.   Like the first little engines, many of our modern locomotives have their own special names.

A modern steam giant

When the last locomotive has moved quietly past us, we make our way with the crowds over the fair grounds. We stop beside one of the late locomotives. We are looking at its shining wheels when the engineer leans out of the window of his little engine house and asks us if we should not like to come up and have a look at the machinery. As we crowd about him, he explains how the giant Steam has been harnessed and made to pull the trains upon which we travel.

"Long, long ago," he says, "men found out that a little steam had enough power to lift things, such as Jamie Watt's tea-kettle lid. They thought to themselves: 'If we could only make a great deal of steam, we should have a great deal of power. We must think out some way to put steam to work for us.' After many tests and trials, and after years of hard work, they invented and improved the steam engine until it has become the good servant that drives our trains and our steamboats for us to-day."

The engineer points out the car just behind his engine. He calls it a *tender*. He says it must go wherever the engine goes, for it carries the tank for the water supply, and the coal or the oil

The engineer leans out of his cab

needed to turn the water into steam. He explains that, for the great locomotives, the water is scooped up into the tender tank from troughs placed here and there between the tracks. These iron horses really drink on the run.

The engineer shows us the great boiler that lies along the backbone of this giant of steel and iron. The fireman opens the door of the fire box and we catch a glimpse of the red flames blazing away inside it. A fireman keeps his engine well fed. A huge iron horse will eat from one and one half to three tons of coal in an hour. Our friend, the engineer, explains that the water in the boiler is heated to boiling by means of a number of pipes that take the heat through it from this fiery furnace. He shows us, too, how the smoke is carried away out of that low smokestack on top of the engine.

What Makes the Engine Go

"This engine of mine is really much like Jamie Watt's teakettle," he says, smiling. "The boiling water in it makes steam which crowds itself into the top of the boiler. The steam tries and tries to get out. But it cannot do so until I open this throttle or faucet. When I push this lever to let the steam out, it moves with a rush. It goes down through those pipes on both sides of the engine. Let us jump down and I will show you just what the steam does."

We climb down from the cab and stand in front of the great wheels. Our engineer friend points to the pipe on this side of the locomotive which brings the steam from the boiler. He shows us how it joins the huge round tube which he calls a *cylinder*. In telling us what the cylinder is for, he says:

"I suppose all you Journey Club boys and girls have bicycles. When your tires are flat, you sometimes use a bicycle pump to fill them with air. The locomotive's cylinder works much like a bicycle pump. Inside it there is a round metal piece which fits close and which moves back and forth. This moving metal piece is a piston like the piston that you force up and down to pump the air into your tires. It is the hot steam rushing from that pipe into the cylinder that pushes this piston from one end

The iron horse drinks on the run

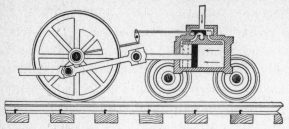

Diagram of simple steam engine

the brakes, and does many other things to make the train safe and comfortable for its passengers."

We are all interested in hearing about locomotives that are run by electricity. We find out that for some railroad work they are better than steam. They do not need coal or fuel oil, and they work all the better in cold weather. They are especially good for going through long close tunnels and for hauling heavy trains over mountains. When going down hill they store away current instead of using it up. Many people like

to the other. The piston in its turn pushes this main rod which, with the help of these side rods, turns the wheels of the engine. It is really steam that sends these great iron horses speeding over the rails with their long trains of freight and passenger cars. Steam also warms the cars, rings the engine bell, pumps the air for

An electric locomotive and train

The locomotive works — where engines are made

them better because they do not make smoke and dirt. Some of the largest of our modern electric engines will do more work than three thousand horses all tugging together.

How a Locomotive Is Built

A two-hour trip in a comfortable day coach and a short taxi ride bring us from the Fair Grounds to our hotel in Philadelphia. Here we stay overnight so that we may visit a locomotive works and see for ourselves how these giant engines are built.

We spend a whole day out at the works on the edge of the city. The manager gives us a guide who takes us first into the designing rooms. Here we see the locomotive born. It first comes to life on the drawing boards of the draftsmen. They draw each one to fit the needs of the railroad for which it is being built. Our heads whirl as we look at the drawings. There are hundreds of parts in an engine, and every one must have its own design.

During our walk through the locomotive works we follow each step of an engine's building from

In the vast boiler shop

the time it leaves the designing room. We see the raw materials brought in on freight cars that run right into the shops. We watch the iron and the steel melted in the roaring furnaces. We stand by the molders who turn the molten metal into all the different parts needed. Then we visit the whirring machines that polish and trim each part until it is perfect.

In the boiler shop we put our hands over our ears, the noise is so great. Here men, wielding clattering machines, are bolting together the steel plates that form the boilers of the engines. At last we come to a vast shed called the erecting shop. Our guide tells us that when an engine leaves the erecting shop it is ready to run. Its boiler is bolted on to its frame and running gear. The fire box is finished. The brakes are set. The cab is placed and every tiny brass fitting is put into position. The bells, the whistle, and the headlight are in working order. Last of all, tests are made to be sure everything is perfect.

Some of our railroads build engines in their own shops. But most have them made to order in

The boiler is bolted to its frame

locomotive works like this. We find that there are many different kinds of engines. Some are built specially for mountain climbing. Others are for passenger trains and still others are planned for hauling long trains of freight cars. One of the heaviest locomotives in the world was built here in these works. It weighed more

A finished locomotive

than eight hundred thousand pounds and it pulled a train of two hundred and fifty-one loaded cars. A heavy freight engine may cost as much as ten to fourteen of our finest automobiles.

Our guide says that American engines are to-day pulling trains in South America, China, and Japan, in Europe, Africa, and far-off Australia, and indeed in all parts of the world.

CHAPTER 9

ON A FAST EXPRESS TRAIN

"We have two hours to wait," Bob says as we enter the railroad station in New York. Later we are to take here a fast express train for Chicago, the greatest railway center of the whole world.

"That will give us time for lunch and a look about this wonderful station," says Mary. Red-capped porters carry our bags to the parcel room. Here, for the sum of ten cents each, we can check our suit

Buying a ticket

cases and umbrellas until we shall want them again.

It is nearly one o'clock and we are hungry. We first make our way to the station dining room, where we sit down at small tables in a restaurant as fine as that of a big hotel. We are able to order the things we like best to eat, and our luncheon is good. When we have finished and have paid our bills, we set forth on our stroll

In a great railroad station

about the great stone station building. We feel very small in its vast main room with the crowds of travelers hurrying to and fro across its marble floors. Our necks almost break as we look up at its ceiling, for this room is as high as a twelve-story house.

At the row of ticket offices at one side, we take our turn with the other travelers. The men in front of us are buying tickets to California, and we hear the woman who follows us say she is going to Texas. The man behind one of the little gratings of the ticket office sells us tiny strips of paper with the words New York and Chicago printed upon them. These are our railroad tickets. At another window not far away we buy Pullman tickets which give us our places in the sleeping car. It seems almost magic to us that these scraps of paper are all we shall need to carry us to Chicago, a thousand miles away.

In a Great Railroad Station

We stroll through several waiting rooms filled with long wooden benches upon which hundreds of people are sitting as they wait for their trains. Jack stops at a telephone booth to call up friends who live in New York. Edith finds a telegraph office where she can send a telegram to her mother. Others of our Club go into the station shops to buy postal cards and gifts to take home. There are many small stores in this huge stone building. There are drug stores, fruit stores, and even stores filled with flowers. There are the rest rooms and wash rooms

There are many trunks in the baggage room

and shoe-shining stands. A porter tells us that there is a well-furnished hospital in case travelers should fall ill and need a doctor or nurse.

One of the most interesting parts of the whole station is the baggage room, with its thousands of trunks. In one section the trunks are all waiting to set forth on their travels to the far corners of our country, and across the wide ocean. In another are trunks ready to be sent out to different parts of the city of New York. Trucks piled high with trunks are rolling past us, some coming in and some going out. We wonder that all these trunks do not get mixed up, but the baggage-master reminds us that each one has tied on its handle a check stamped with the name of the city to which it is to go and a number by which its owner may claim it. We have often checked our own trunks from one place to another in our longer Journey Club tours.

In this station building are the offices of many of the railroad officials. The men who direct the trains, who tell them what tracks they shall use and when they shall use them are all hard at work here. They signal the trains by means of electric switch-boards, by telephone or telegraph.

When we come again to the main room of the station, we stop at the information desk and find that our train will leave from track number seven. At the news stand we buy a few magazines to help pass the time while we are on the train, and then we call red-capped porters to help us again with our heavy bags which we have claimed at the check-room.

A lighted sign high above us tells us our train is now ready. With

A parcel room check

a crowd of other passengers we go down to the gates to the tracks. How many of these tracks there are! A trainman near our gate tells us there is room upon the tracks of this station for more than one thousand cars. He says that this is one of

At the information desk

the two biggest railway stations in the world, and that thirty thousand travelers can be taken care of here without too much crowding.

Here is track seven! We stop at its iron gate to have our tickets looked at and punched by the gate-man. And then we hurry along down the platform to our car, whose number we know from our Pullman tickets.

All Aboard!

"Board! All abo-a-r-d!"
The conductor calls this out several times in a loud voice as we are settling ourselves in our seats in the sleeping car. A few last-minute travelers come breathlessly in, and the train moves slowly out of the station.

All aboard!

A Pullman porter in a white coat helps us to put our baggage out of the way under the seats. He brings paper bags to protect the hats of the girls from the dust,

A Pullman car with a berth made up

and he says we may have pillows when we wish to lie back to rest.

What a beautiful car this Pullman is! At first we think its shining walls are of wood. But when Dick taps upon them with his pencil we find they are really

of steel, painted and polished to look like fine wood. The porter says that in accidents steel is safer than wood, which is apt to fly into splinters. Then, too, steel lasts much longer than wood.

Helen is running her hand over the soft plush of the seats. Indeed, this car is just a parlor on wheels. Its floor is covered with a soft blue carpet, and pretty lamps are set in its ceiling. Through its broad windows we can look out at the countryside as we roll along over the rails. The car is warm and comfortable. It is heated by steam, and yet the air is good. There are little windows in the roof to let fresh air in, and we can also open slots in the base of our windows if we should find it too hot.

The seats in our cars are arranged in pairs facing each other. We find that each pair makes what is called a section. Between the sections there are headboards that run from the seat-backs up to the roof so that we are somewhat shut off from our next neighbors. As we entered the car we walked past a little room for travelers who wish to be entirely off by themselves. We like the open sections better, for we think they have more air, and then too we enjoy watching our fellow passengers as they come and go.

Private rooms like that at the end of our car are called drawing-rooms or compartments. They cost a little more than places in the open part of the car. The porter tells us that some Pullman cars have nothing but compartments and drawing-rooms. These drawing rooms and compartments may each have places for two or three persons. A few trains are made up of rooms in which there is only one single bed instead of regular berths. Single room cars are generally used for short overnight trips.

We remember other short trips which we have made in Pullman parlor cars and in day coaches.

The parlor cars are filled with soft plush-covered chairs that turn on bases of iron. Some of the newest of the day coaches are almost as fine as a Pullman car. They have comfortable

In a single room

seats covered with plush and they are handsomely decorated. A day coach has room for three times as many passengers as a Pullman.

Here come the railroad and the Pullman conductors! They punch our tickets to show that

Seats are comfortable in parlor cars

they have been examined and then give them back to us.

As we look about us, we think how different this car is from the ones on which we have traveled in Europe. The cars there are smaller than ours and each is divided into compartments with places for six or eight travelers. Sometimes these compartments are built to open off a long hall that runs the length of the car.

Others have doors that open on the outside of the car. Before the train starts the trainmen lock all the doors tight. They unlock them again when it pulls into a station.

European sleeping compartments have berths for one or two persons, and between each pair of rooms there is a small dressing room. Such sleeping cars can carry only half as many passengers as the one we are riding in. On many European trains there are first, second, and third-class cars. To ride in the more comfortable first and second-class cars costs a good deal more than in the third-class cars with their hard wooden seats.

best and finest trains in the United States and it costs more to ride upon it than on an ordinary slower and less comfortable one.

Foreign trains have compartments that open on the side

An All-Pullman Train

During the afternoon we walk through our long train from one end to the other. As we leave our car, Dick says:

"Don't forget that the name of our car is *Point Airy*. There are so many sleeping cars just like it on this train that we may have trouble in finding our sections again."

Our train is an all-Pullman train. It has no day coaches such as we have taken for our shorter trips. This is one of the

This train goes at a speed of fifty miles and more an hour. It is called a *Limited*, for only a limited number of tickets for the train are sold each day. The conductor says so many persons want to go on this train that it has to run in several sections. There are two other trains just as fine and as long as ours,

There is even a secretary

following close behind us on the rails.

We make our way through one sleeper after another. Each is filled with people reading, or talking as they sit looking out of the windows. In one or two sections the porters have set up little tables so that the passengers can play cards or write letters. One car is a diner where we shall have dinner later on, and at the very end of the train we find the observation car with its wide plate glass windows and its huge easy chairs. Some of the people here are reading its magazines and newspapers. That man at the desk in the corner is a stenographer, who may be engaged to write letters on his typewriter. In another car we find a bathroom with a real tub and a shower, and a barber shop where a traveler is having his hair cut. We may even have our clothes pressed while we are asleep. The porter tells us of other trains upon which he has served where they have radio concerts, a gymnasium, and a special car for moving pictures and dances. These, he says, are for longer journeys than ours.

Now our train is going around a hairpin curve. It is so sharp that we can see the front end of our train with its puffing locomotive and its tender behind. This was later exchanged for the steam horse that is pulling us now. Those cars just behind the tender are the mail and baggage cars. We heard of such a postoffice on

The dining car is like a fine restaurant

The city of New York does not allow engines that burn coal or oil to come into its stations with their smoke and their cinders. Our train was pulled out of the city by a clean electric engine. wheels in "The Story of a Stamp" during our trips to find out about ourselves and our city. The baggage cars of our train are filled to the doors with trunks and boxes and other things that have

In the club car

been either checked by the passengers or sent by an express company.

As we came from one car to another, we walked through little inclosed passages called vestibules. These sleepers are all vestibule cars. They are much safer than the cars that have nothing to shield the passengers as they step from the platform of one car to another.

The porter opens the door of the observation car so that we may go out and sit down in chairs on the little platform at the very end of our train. As we watch the miles of smooth track unroll behind us, some one recites a verse written by John G. Saxe. It goes:

" Swinging through the forests,
     Battling over ridges,
 Shooting under arches,
     Rumbling over bridges,
 Whizzing through the mountains,
     Buzzing o'er the vale,
 Bless me, this is pleasant,
     Riding on the Rail ! "

A Good Night's Sleep

We eat our dinner at small tables on each side of the aisle of the dining car. We are served by men in white coats who bring from the kitchen the delicious dishes we have ordered from the menu card.

When we reach our own sleeper, *Point Airy*, we find that the porter is just beginning to make up one of our *lower berths*. See, he is pulling out the seat cushions until they meet each other. He next slides down the cushions from the seat-backs to fill the spaces thus left. The whole makes a fine wide bed. One cushioned head-rest he pulls up to make a place for us to lay our clothes.

Now with a twist of his wrist he unlocks and pulls down a broad shelf which has been hidden away in the sloping roof of the car. This is another bed, or the *upper berth* as he calls it. Upon it he finds piled mattresses, pillows, and blankets for both the berths.

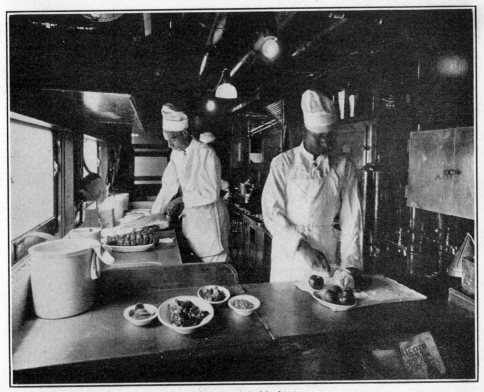

In the train's kitchen

We rumble over bridges

We speed around a curve

car for pillowcases and sheets. In a very few minutes he has made up the two berths into beds almost as comfortable as those we sleep in at home. The fixed headboards between the sections separate the berths from their neighbors. In some of the older cars which did not have these partitions, thin boards were slipped in between the berths to serve the same purpose. He shows us how

We watch him as he goes to the tiny closet in one end of the

Watching the scenery from the observation platform

Tunnels are made through the hills

the heavy green cloth curtains shut each berth away from the sight of persons in the aisles of the car. He tells us to be sure to remember the numbers upon our own curtains lest we should crawl into the wrong berths when we come back from the dressing rooms.

"Oh, but I'm sleepy," Edith says, yawning. "I think I'll go to bed right away." The rest of us decide to follow her example. The girls take their tooth brushes and other toilet articles down to the women's dressing room at one end of the car and the boys go to the men's room at the other end. When the porter has made up all our berths, we tumble in. We giggle and laugh as some of us climb up a little stepladder into the uppers, and we each button the curtains of our berth together behind us. The porter shows us the bells in the walls of our berths and says we are to ring if we should want him during the night.

People have not always been able to travel so comfortably as we can to-day. When they went on long journeys in the early days of the railroads, they used to sit up all night in the day coaches. A few sleeping cars had already been tried when George M. Pullman became interested and built the first Pullman sleeper less than one hundred years ago. The very earliest forefather of our *Point Airy* found but four passengers willing to pay an extra amount to sleep while they traveled. Its berths had mattresses and pillows but no sheets or pillowcases. Its only light came from flickering candles and its dressing room consisted of a single wash basin in the end of the car.

In those early days there were many short railroads. In going from Albany to Buffalo, travelers rode on seven railroads and they had to change cars six times during the trip. Later many of the roads joined together to make one whole. To-day our railroads are grouped into several great systems.

A Talk with a Railroad Builder

When we come back to our seats after an early breakfast next morning our berths are out of sight, and the car looks just as it did when we came aboard. We find a pleasant-faced man sitting in one of our sections. His berth has not yet been put away and he has no other place to sit. We make him welcome and fall to talking with him about the wonderful journey we are having.

"I wonder if you boys and girls know of all the work and the planning that has been necessary

An open car for livestock

to make your trip possible," he says with a smile. "I am a railroad man. My job is to lay out and build railroads just like this. If you like, I will tell you a little about it. A new railroad is built through parts of our country where there are people living who have no means of traveling or of getting the things they raise or make to the market. Or perhaps it is built because a certain section could be well used for farms or for factories if there was only

a way to get the people into it. When we have decided where a railroad is needed, we send out our experts to lay out the route where there are the fewest hills.

"You see, to pull trains up hill needs lots of coal," the railroad builder explains, "and to go fast, trains must have as level a track as possible. It is for these reasons that we cut through the hills and fill in the little valleys wherever we can. That, too, is why we build level bridges over deep valleys as well as over rivers, and why our steam shovels are put to work to burrow long tunnels through the high mountains."

Our new friend tells us that dirt roadbeds are not firm enough to bear the weight of heavy trains. Deep layers of crushed rock must be laid on the dirt so that the rains cannot wash the roadbed away. Upon these roads of rock are placed crossties of wood or sometimes of steel and to them the shining steel rails of the tracks are spiked or bolted down. Last of all comes the building of stations to shelter the passengers and their baggage, and warehouses for sorting the freight.

Our Friend, the Freight Car

As we speed along toward Chicago we pass many other trains.

We wonder what all these freight cars are carrying. Some are open so that we can see their loads. Here are some flat cars loaded with lumber and stone and heavy machinery. Hitched

Many workmen are needed to lay the steel tracks

Our railroad-builder friend tells us Chicago is the greatest railroad center of the whole world. Thirty-nine different roads end their tracks in its huge union stations. Every day there roll into its freight yards cars from each one of our forty-eight states.

behind them are several tank cars filled with gasoline and fuel oil. These open cars heaped up with coal are gondola cars and hopper cars, and that one we are passing now is a refrigerator car. Refrigerator cars are chilled with ice and they have tight double

We inspect a refrigerator freight car [Bob, Dick, Helen, Jack, Mary, and Edith]

doors to keep the cold in. Ice-boxes on wheels like these bring us much of our meat and our fruit, our vegetables and our butter and eggs.

The doors of the box cars are tightly closed. The railroad man says that every sort of food and clothing and the other things we need in our daily life are carried over the country in box cars like these. He explains that many of these freight cars are of steel, or of wood with ends of steel. In the olden days all freight cars were made of wood. They were not so strong as those of to-day.

Now we are passing cars filled with animals. The mooing of the cows and the squeals of the pigs can be heard as we go by. Edith almost thinks she is at home again on her father's farm. Stock cars are specially built for cattle and horses, for sheep and for pigs. The animals can be fed and watered right in the cars and they get plenty of air through the open slat sides.

"The freight car is the farmer's best friend," says our seat-mate. "Without freight cars to carry his wares to the big markets, he could not sell his crops or his

cattle so well. It is the same with our factories. They must have the faithful freight car to bring them their fuel and the materials with which they work, and to take their wares to the

Track walkers inspect every inch of rail

stores all over our land. The motor truck helps greatly for short journeys, but it is not so good for very long trips. Indeed, the freight car is the good friend as well of the Journey Club's members and all the rest of the people who live in our country. Almost everything you eat, wear, or use has traveled by freight at some time or other."

Who Runs Our Railroads for Us

"It must take many men to run all our railroads," Jack says to the railroad man.

"Indeed it does," is his answer. "Thousands upon thousands! You have already found out about the men in the iron mines and the steel mills, the engine builders and the workmen in the car-building works. In the railroad companies themselves, you must think of the thousands of hands that are needed to make the roads and lay the tracks. You must think of the presidents and managers and secretaries and clerks who direct the work of all these others. You must not forget the engineers and the fire-

Iron horses ready to speed away into the night

men on the locomotives, and the conductors, brakemen, and trainmen on the express trains and locals that run over the rails in every part of our land. Then there are the men in the railroad repair shops, in the engine houses, and at the railway crossings. A great railroad has many men who do nothing but walk the tracks to see that every bolt and rail is in perfect shape. This helps to prevent accidents, for a foot of track out of order may wreck a fast train and injure or kill those riding upon it. In addition to all these, there are the ticket agents and the baggage masters, the mechanics and the men and women who keep the cars and stations clean. Almost two million men and women are employed by our railroads.

As we think of these people who are helping us to travel, we see again how we all depend on each other. We find that each one has his own special part in doing the work of the world and in making his neighbor's life run more smoothly.

The Journey Club rides in a taxicab to see the sights of Washington, D. C.

CHAPTER 10

WE TRAVEL ABOUT OUR OWN CITY

"Is every one here?" Helen asks as we gather in front of her house. Our next Journey Club trip will not take us far. We are glad, for we are tired with our long trip over the railroads. To-day we are to travel upon another kind of a railroad. It is so different from the great steam railroads that often we do not think of its being a railroad at all. It is the street railroad that goes through our city from one end to the other. It does not run by steam but its cars depend on steel rails just as do the fast express trains that rush over our land at such a great speed.

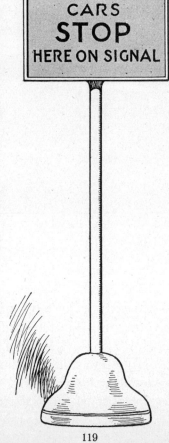

We start briskly off down the street to the nearest street car line. We wait a few minutes under the little sign that tells us where the cars stop. Here comes one going in our direction as we know by the sign on it. The motorman waits while we climb up a few steps into the car. We have our fares ready. Some of us use little metal pieces called *car-tokens*. Others pay in real money. In some places paper tickets are used.

The rush hour is over, and there are plenty of empty seats for us in this street car. As we ride we look out of its broad windows at the streets with their streams of automobiles and motor trucks. Many people who wish to go about our city ride in taxicabs or automobiles. But our streets are so crowded that it is often hard to find parking space.

At the Car Barns

"Clang! Clang! Get out of my way!" says the bell of the street car when some automobile or wagon runs along in front of it on its tracks. We ride on and on through one busy street after

Where street cars spend the night

Many times it is easier to take a street car than to use our automobiles. Then, too, there are many of us who cannot afford to own motor cars, and riding in taxicabs costs a good deal. The distances are great here in our city, so we must have some cheap way of riding from one part of it to the other.

another. We stop every so often to let passengers off and to take others on. Now we have reached the edge of the town where the houses are few.

"End of the route," the conductor calls out as our car comes to a halt. We file through its front door and find ourselves just outside the car barns where the street cars of this line are housed. A maze of tracks and switches leads into the great sheds. As we peer into these we see that there are a number of cars standing still on the tracks, waiting until they shall be needed.

At the office we find the man in charge. His name is Mr. Gregg. He is very obliging and offers to show us around the car barns himself. He walks with us through the sheds and tells us many interesting things about these street railways of ours.

"You should come out here in the early morning before the sun rises," Mr. Gregg says with a smile. "That's a busy time, I can tell you. These barns are filled to their very doors, for this is where our cars spend the night. The last one is put to bed long after midnight, but even then there is no rest for the poor street cars. An army of car cleaners pounces down upon

them with buckets and brushes, brooms and dusters. When at last all the cars have been made neat and tidy, it is nearly time to think of the runs for the next

A crowded city street car

day. Our conductors and motormen often come to work while it is yet dark. The yardmen bring out the cars for them and soon, one after another, they hurry off to the city.

"Our first riders are laborers and porters and factory folk. Later we take in the clerks and the men and women who work in our offices and our stores. Our very busiest hours are these morning hours when people are going to their work, and again in the late afternoon when they come home again. At other times of the day there are not so many people who want to ride, so we do not need all our cars. They wait here in the barns until a busy hour comes again."

City Travel of Other Days

The chief reason why people need street cars is to take them to and from their work. In the

A fine old omnibus

early days our now thriving city was a small town. Its stores and its houses were close together. Its people could easily walk to any part of the town. But as the years went by, more and more men and women came to live and work here. Our town grew bigger and bigger. It became a small city. Those whose homes were in its

newer parts found that they could not walk the long distances to their places of business. So they began to think up ways in which they might ride.

"My father was a street car man before me," says Mr. Gregg. "He drove one of the very first street cars in the United States. He has told me many interesting stories of the ways city people traveled in those early days. The first way of all was by the old-fashioned omnibus. This was just like an overgrown stagecoach. It could carry perhaps a dozen or even more passengers, and its horses had to pull hard to get it over the hills. It ran from the railway station to the public square of the town where the only hotel was, sometimes a very long ride over poor streets. The streets then were so rough that the travelers were jolted this way and that."

Mr. Gregg's father drove one of the early horse cars that came just after the omnibus. We have already found out how our fore-fathers learned to make cars that would run on the rails of the first railroads. People soon began to think of trying such steam cars for city travel as well. But with the streets so full of horses and carriages and people walking about, it would not have been safe to use puffing steam engines. Then, too, their smoke and their cinders would have been most unpleasant. So the first real street cars were drawn over the rails by teams of stout horses. Mr. Gregg says his father's car had red curtains at its windows. It was lighted by a smoky kerosene lamp. It was very crude, but still it could go so much faster and so much more smoothly than the old omnibus that people were glad to ride in it.

An early horse car

The Cable Car

In our country there is much work to be done. We do not like to waste time. We do not walk when we can ride, and we are always trying to find ways to get from one place to another more quickly. These horse-drawn cars were not fast enough for the people of our busy cities, and soon the cable car was invented. This was about sixty years ago.

Mr. Gregg says that the cable car was pulled along by a strong steel cable that ran under the street. The car was hooked on the cable line by a steel clamp called a *grip*. This steel clamp ran from the bottom of the car through a slot in a trench dug down under the street, where it gripped the steel rope that formed the cable. The cable was kept moving through this trench by a giant spool called a *drum* placed in the engine house at the end of the route. A steam engine there kept the drum turning all the time.

When the cable car driver opened his grip by means of a lever, the cable slipped through it and the car stopped. When he clamped his grip down gently, the cable would slip only a little and the car would go slowly. But when the clamp gripped the cable rope tight, the car would be pulled along at the rate of eight or ten miles an hour.

Cars That Run by Electricity

"How delighted we all were when the first electric car ran," says this street car man. During our trips to find out about the houses we live in, the Journey Club has heard about electricity and the many wonderful things it does for us. Mr. Gregg says the first electric cars were trolley cars. He shows us one of the trolley cars that are used on the line that goes from here through the suburbs of our city. He points out the trolley wires that run on poles high over the track. He says they carry electric current made by whirling dynamos in the power house not far away. He shows us how the long iron pole on the roof of the car, with its little wheel running along touching the wires, brings

One of the first electric street cars

the electric current into the car's motor and makes the wheels turn.

Bob has seen another kind of a trolley car. It has a tall framework of steel and copper built on its roof. A certain part of this metal frame touches the wire with its electric current and so brings the power into the motor.

The electric street car in which

we came out here to-day is not just like these trolley cars. It gets its power from a third rail that runs in a steel tube down under the street. Wires from the power house keep this third rail well supplied with the powerful electric current it needs to send the street, it would kill any one who might touch it by accident. Trolley wires are used only for street cars in the less crowded towns or in the suburbs of the big cities.

Mr. Gregg tells us that these beautiful electric cars cost many

A modern trolley car

these heavy street cars speeding over the rails. Third rails under the street are better for busy streets than wires. So many poles and wires overhead spoil the beauty of our city. They get in the way of the tall ladders of our fire department when they are fighting a fire. Then, too, live electric wires are dangerous. If one should break and fall to times as much as the old-fashioned horse cars. But he says too that they are easier to run and cheaper to keep going. They do not get tired, they do not have to have food and water, and they can go many times faster. Some street cars need only one man to run them. In these every one enters by the front door and the motor-man acts also as conductor.

Our national capital has fine motor busses and streets

During the busiest hours there must be cars with conductors also.

A Motor Bus Ride

"You should take one of our motor busses back to town," says Mr. Gregg. "Motor busses have been found so valuable for carrying people about city streets that many street car companies like ours, and other private companies, too, run regular lines. Busses do not need rails. They can go through parts of the city where street cars do not run. More and more motor busses are being used every year."

As the motor bus line starts not far from these car barns, we decide to follow Mr. Gregg's advice. There are several kinds of motor busses. There are some that look like giant automobile sedans with two rows of seats

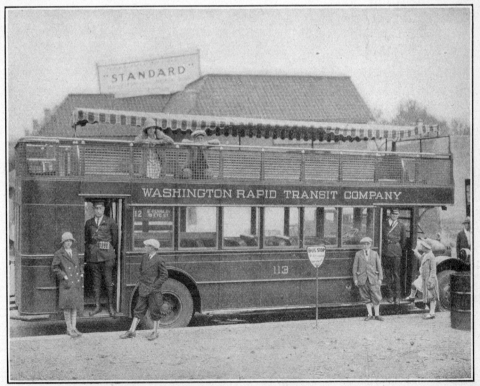

We take a bus [Mary, Jack, Helen, Bob, Dick, and Edith]

Busses have soft seats

especially pleasant on bright sunny days like this. Upon two-story busses there is a conductor as well as a driver.

The busses of this line are handsome cars painted in beautiful colors. Their seats are of leather and they are almost as comfortable to ride in as a fine motor car. As they roll smoothly along on their giant tires filled with air, we think we like riding in them even better than in the street cars. To ride in a motor bus usually costs a little more.

inside them like those of a street car. A driver in uniform sits at the wheel and takes up the fares as the passengers enter. Others have also seats on their roofs. These two-story busses are

A fleet of busses ready for duty

CHAPTER 11

HOW THREE NEW YORKERS WENT HOME

Our Club is meeting again this afternoon. During our stay at the car barns, Mr. Gregg told us of a moving picture which he thought we really should see. So we have come down to the theater where it is being shown.

This picture tells us how people travel in the great city of New York. We first see the streams of automobiles and motor busses speeding in four lines, and sometimes more, over broad Fifth Avenue. Then we watch crowds of people getting on and off street cars that go from one side of the city to another. Now comes a section that shows us how three different men who

The three New Yorkers

work in New York ride to their homes at the end of the day.

The first man's name seems to be Mr. Thomas. We follow him as he leaves his huge office building and hurries along the sidewalk to an iron stairway. This stairway leads to a platform built high above the busy street. Masses of iron and steel supports rise over the street like a railway bridge. This is a part of the Elevated Railway, or the "L," as most people call it. Our film shows Mr. Thomas crowding with many others into one of the cars. Now he is whizzing along over the rails. He can look right into the open

129

windows of the houses he passes, for the "L" runs most of the time on a level with their second stories. The first elevated trains were pulled by steam engines. These were noisy and dirty, so, as soon as it was possible, the engines were given up and cleaner and quieter electric motors were placed in the cars.

down many steps. This is the entrance to a subway station, and Mr. Richards is on his way to take a train that runs on rails through tunnels down under the streets. He stops at a little

On the way to work along Fifth Avenue in New York

On the Subway

Our second New Yorker's name is Mr. Richards. He walks rapidly along the street to a doorway on the corner. He goes gate to drop his fare into the fare box. This opens the gate and he hurries on with the crowds. What a huge platform this is upon which he is standing! The words on the screen tell us it is several blocks long. Its walls are made up of small tiles, and iron railings on its platform's edge keep back the crowds. The subway station is clean and brightly lighted. There are hundreds of other people waiting here for their trains. Subways like this run under many parts of New York, and their speeding trains carry millions of people up and down town every twenty-four hours. They go at all hours of the day and the night.

Here comes a train! Every second car has electric motors that send their wheels spinning along on the rails. The cars are filled to the very doors with people on their way home from work. Mr. Richards first takes an express car that makes but few stops. This runs on a separate track from the locals. There are no crossings on these underground railways and the express trains can go very fast without danger. As he nears his home district, our traveler changes to a local train which stops at each station.

It costs millions of dollars to build elevated railroads and subways like these. We wonder that subways can have been dug without the streets above giving way and all the buildings

Workers coming up out of the subway

falling down. But the digging was done with the greatest of care. Huge machines ate their way little by little into the earth. As soon as the first hole was made, the engineers set up heavy steel supports and built a strong steel or wood ceiling. The digging machines were put to work again to eat away a little more of the earth. More steel props and more strong ceilings were set, and so on and on, digging and ceiling, until at last the vast tunnels were finished. In some places the broader streets were opened and as New York, Chicago, Boston, and Philadelphia that have elevated trains or subways.

Roads under a River

In New York there are also other tunnels that seem even

A subway train at the station platform

great trenches dug through them. When these were roofed over with their ceilings, the streets were replaced.

It costs millions of dollars to run elevated trains and subways like these. Only very large cities have enough travelers to pay for their building and for keeping them going. It is cities such more wonderful to us than these subways that run down under the streets. These are the tunnels that have been bored through the muddy floors of the wide rivers that flow by the city. Their steel tubes are big enough to allow railroad trains to pass through them. They save travelers the trouble of crossing the rivers on the slower ferryboats.

The third of our New Yorkers lives across the Hudson River in New Jersey. His name is Mr. Henry. The screen tells us that some distance from the great store where he works. Now he is driving carefully through the traffic towards the North River, as this lower part of the Hudson River is often called.

An elevated train

until just lately he took the trains in the subway and went through the tubes under the river to get to his home. But when we see Mr. Henry now, he is stepping into his automobile. He has left his car all day in a garage "Guess how he will get across!" says the film. We think we know the answer, for we ourselves have ridden in automobiles to the Jersey shore. They were carried across the water on ferryboats. But we are wrong. "He will

Automobiles on a ferry

drive over a road that goes under the river through the Holland Tunnel," the screen's words inform us. And indeed that is the wonderful way Mr. Henry goes home.

The Holland Tunnel was built only a short time ago. Its two giant tubes lie bedded deep in the muddy floor of the river that separates New York from its neighbor, New Jersey. One of the tubes is for automobiles going west. The other is for cars that wish to go east. Our trav-

eler, Mr. Henry, stops near the entrance to pay his toll charge and then drives on down the tunnel at a speed of about thirty miles an hour.

How light it is away down there under the river! The walls of the tunnel are of shining white tiles. There are brilliant electric lights every few yards. Traffic policemen stand along the way to keep the cars moving. They are helped in their task by red and green signal lights like those in our big business

Inside the Holland Tunnel under the Hudson River

section down town. We are told that the air is kept pure by giant fans that blow fresh air into the tunnels through holes in the curbs. These also take away the bad odors and the dangerous gases from the automobile engines. Nearly fifty thousand cars go through the Holland Tunnel in one day.

CHAPTER 12

AN AUTOMOBILE TRIP

One morning more than thirty years ago crowds gathered along a certain street in New York. Men, women, and children stood on tiptoe and craned their necks. They wanted to catch a glimpse of the wonderful new "horseless carriage" that was to be tried out. They did not believe that a carriage could actually run by itself. They thought the tales they had heard were just foolish jokes.

A horseless carriage

But soon, with a clattering noise and a cloud of bad-smelling smoke pouring out of its back, the "horseless carriage" came by. The crowds gasped in wonder. Among them on the curb was a Chinese man, his slant eyes opened wide with surprise. As he stared, he cried out in a loud voice: "Oh! Oh! No pushee! No pullee! All samee, go like windee!"

That was one of the very first automobiles that ran on the streets of an American city. The automobile was really born across the ocean in Europe. Its name comes from two foreign words. *Auto* means "self," and *mobile* means "movable." So automobile is just a short way of saying "a vehicle that moves by itself." The English use the name motor car instead of automobile for their self-movable carriages.

136

The first automobiles of all were run by steam. At the Fair of the Iron Horse we heard of steam road carriages that were built in France and in England more than one hundred years ago. They were heavy clumsy affairs. They were like giant stagecoaches with steam engines built in them

An early steam road carriage

to make their wheels turn. The English people feared these strange steam road carriages and laws were passed against them. One of these laws said that every self-moving carriage must have a man walk before it waving a red flag to warn the people of the dangerous machine that was coming. Such automobiles were forbidden to go at a speed of more than four miles an hour.

"Who invented automobiles like ours?" Jack asks this question as we discuss to-day's journey to find out about the motor cars that carry us so quickly and comfortably on our travels. No one can answer him. We know who invented the steam locomotive. We know who invented the cotton gin and the sewing machine. But the automobile was the work of many men, not of just one. Frenchmen and Germans, Englishmen and Americans all helped to make for us the beautiful cars we ride in to-day. Perhaps we owe most to Captain Cugnot in France who built the first steam road carriage. Or perhaps to Carl Benz of Germany who made the first motor car that used gasoline. Or, indeed, perhaps most important of all was that cave man who hewed out the first wheel so long ago.

The travels we begin to-day are to be entirely by automobile. We have chosen Detroit, the biggest automobile city of the whole world, as the end of our journey. And we have decided to make our trip there in the comfortable automobile busses that run over the smooth roads between our big cities. We shall stop off at night at good hotels, taking new busses each morning as we go on with our trip. Although we may use a little more time in this way, we shall ride quite as comfortably as if we were traveling on a fast train.

Early American Automobiles

As we wait for the time for the automobile bus to depart, we chat with its driver. He is a man about as old as our own fathers. He says he has been interested in motor cars since their very earliest days. He knows many stories about the first American automobiles.

"Away back in 1892," he begins, "a certain man who lived in Massachusetts spent all the time he could get in an old stable. He worked day and night. His friends laughed when he told them he was trying to build a gasoline automobile. They did not think he could do it. But at last his strange-looking horseless

The Journey Club travels by motor bus [Jack, Mary, Helen, Edith, and Dick]

carriage was finished. With fear in his heart, he brought it out for a trial. As he was turning its crank, the car began to move rapidly. Crash! It ran away into the side of the barn. It was almost wrecked, but its builder was delighted; for its running away only proved that the engine he had made would turn the wheels of his automobile. This man's name was Charles Duryea, and this horseless carriage of his was the first American gasoline car that really ran. He called it the 'Buggy-aut.'"

"Then perhaps Duryea was the inventor of our American automobiles," Mary says.

"No" is the reply. "He has often been called the Father of the American Automobile, but there were many other men working too at this same time and the automobiles they finished soon after his ran quite as well as the Buggy-aut. Henry Ford drove his first car just a little later and several others appeared on the city streets riding in the automobiles

they had built. Since then, many hundreds and thousands of inventors have worked to make our motor cars better. I could not begin to tell you all the names of even the most important."

Henry Ford in his first automobile

At first just a few automobiles were made each year. These cost so much that only the very rich could afford them. But when it was seen what wonderful servants automobiles could be, more and more people wanted them. Carriage and wagon-builders and other factory owners turned to building these new horseless carriages. They learned to make them better and better. They put up huge factories and made special tools.

In the beginning the builders worked chiefly to improve their engines. They wanted to be sure their automobiles would run and not break down. When something went wrong and the engine their engines, they studied to make the bodies more comfortable and more beautiful. To-day our automobiles are truly small palaces on wheels. Emperors and kings of the olden times never dreamed of such ease and luxury in riding as we can buy now at a very low price. As the factories

Italy   France   Canada   England   United States

The United States has two hundred times as many automobiles as Italy

stopped on the road, an unkind passer-by was sure to call out with a jeering voice, "Get a horse! Get a horse!" One company advertised its car, "built to go and keep going." Those early cars were noisy and smelly, and many people made fun of them. In an English magazine, this verse was printed:

" What rushes through the crowded
     street
   With whirring noise and throbbing
     beat,
   Exhaling odors far from sweet,
     The motor car!"

When at last the automobile makers felt they could depend on learned to make automobiles in vast numbers, they found they could sell them more cheaply. In our land almost every family that is comfortably off owns an automobile. Some have two or even more.

What the Automobile Does for Us

Now we have started. We roll along over the smooth streets of our city and over a hard broad highway out into the country. As we ride along in our bus we decide to play one of our favorite games. We divide ourselves into two sides, the girls against the boys. We take turns and each time our names are called we tell of some way in which the automobile helps us. Jack speaks of the trucks that deliver our coal. Edith says much of our milk and many of our vegetables are brought into our city from

Trucks bring in our milk every day

farms in the country by auto trucks. Helen tells of the cars that help bring us our mail, while Bob reminds us that all our fire engines now are automobiles. Dick mentions the motor snowplows that clear our city streets in the winter time; and other members of our club tell of the many different packages that are delivered at our doors, by automobile or truck from the stores of our city.

Meat, books, groceries, and clothing, and indeed almost all things that we use every day are brought to us by the automobile.

Mary thinks that one of the very nicest ways in which the automobile serves us is in the pleasure it gives us to ride

Trucks carry our vegetables

Many trucks were used in the World War

about through the country. As we look out of the windows of our speeding coach at the trees and the fields, at the tiny towns and the cities, we think she is right. In an afternoon's motor ride we can go ten times as far as our grandmothers and grandfathers could drive with their horses and carriages of the past. As we loll back in our comfortable cushioned seats, going along so fast and so smoothly, we do not wonder that all the world wants to ride in an automobile.

A little more than thirty years ago all the cars made in one year in the United States could be counted on the fingers of your two hands. Now they roll out of our factories by the millions. Last year enough cars were built to make five lines all the way from Boston on the

Atlantic Ocean to Seattle on the Pacific. And there are so many cars running over our roads to-day that if they were all divided up equally, there would be one for almost every family in the United States.

In our country there live only one fourteenth of all the people of the earth. But of every ten automobiles in the world, eight belong to us. We make the most and we use the most. The United States owns more than twenty-two times as many motor cars as does any other nation. Yet little by little the automobile is making its way into the far corners of the world. Camel caravans on the desert often meet motor cars filled with tourists and travelers. China, Japan, Siam, and India, and indeed all nations now have automobiles running upon the streets of their big cities.

Helen's Uncle Harry fought in the World War. He has often told her the thrilling story of how automobile taxicabs saved the city of Paris in 1914. In one night the brave taxi-drivers and their sturdy cars took many thousands of soldiers to the battle-fields forty miles away, so that at sunrise the next morning the German army might be driven back. Helen says automobiles and trucks were used at many other times and places during this war. They brought tons of food to the troops. They drew heavy guns. There were automobile ambulances that carried the wounded back to the

An automobile ambulance

hospitals. There were movable motor-kitchens, and motor cycles and side cars for hurrying messengers. Generals and captains, lieutenants and privates all rode in automobiles when they wanted to go quickly from one place to another along the fighting fronts.

What Makes the Wheels Go Round?

"Steam automobiles were the most popular at first," our bus driver explains as we chat with him at the end of our day's ride. They were so quiet and so easy to run. But they were dangerous, too. There was always the fear of fire from their flames. And the water in their boilers was apt to freeze in cold weather. So when the gasoline engine came, the steam engine was gradually pushed to one side."

"What makes our car go?" Dick asks. "I know how the steam of the steam engine pushes the pistons that turn the wheels of the great locomotive. And I know that this car of ours burns gasoline. But I don't see any cylinders or pistons and I should like to know what makes these wheels of ours turn around."

"Well, the cylinders and the pistons are there, even though you can't see them now," the driver says. "The great secret

We get gasoline at a filling station [Bob, Dick, and Jack]

of our engine is in its food, gasoline.

"Do you boys and girls know where gasoline comes from?" Indeed, we do. We well remember our trip to the oil lands in our this crude oil to the refineries. During our visit to such a refinery we saw how the petroleum was cooked and cooled and turned into gasoline, kerosene, and other oil products.

Petroleum wells furnish crude oil

journeys to find out about the houses we live in. We remember watching the great drills boring their way down, down into the earth to get the oil out. We have seen the crude oil, or petroleum, as it comes forth from the wells. It is thick and dark. It is not at all like the clear gasoline we buy for our automobiles at the filling stations. We remember the pipe lines that run under the ground for many miles to carry

The driver lifts up the hood of the bus to show us the engine. He explains its workings to us. He tells us how the gasoline runs from the tank through the feed pipe; how it becomes mixed with air and turned into a spray in the carburetor; and how from there the air and gas are drawn into the cylinders. He explains how the mixture of air and gasoline is squeezed inside each little tube-like cylinder, and how at just the right moment it is lighted by an electric spark. We all know how easily gasoline will explode. When the electric spark touches the gas, there is a tiny explosion inside the cylinder. This the crank-shaft. As the pistons are moved down, one after another, by the series of small explosions of the lighted gas and air mixture, they turn the crank-shaft; the crank-shaft turns the

Gasoline drives us swiftly along

pushes a little piston much as the steam pushed the giant piston in the locomotive's great cylinder.

"The ends of this little piston and of its brother pistons from the other cylinders of the engine are fastened to a long steel rod that is connected with the back wheels of the automobile. This rod is wheels around and around; and the car speeds ahead.

"The first automobiles had but one or two cylinders," the bus driver says. "But now most of our cars have four or six and larger ones may have eight or even twelve cylinders." We watch our friend fill his radiator with water. His engine would become much too hot if it were not for the water jacket that surrounds it and the whirling fan that keeps the water cool. One make of automobile cools its engine with air. A special fan sends the air in as the car goes along.

There is one other kind of automobile, but it is not so much used now as in earlier days. This is the automobile that runs by electricity. It is cleaner and quieter and easier to drive than a gasoline car. But it cannot go so far, for its electric battery is very heavy and it has only enough current to last for a short distance. It must be given new current often and this takes a good while. The electric automobile must move more slowly, too. It seldom has a speed

Some cars run by electricity

of more than twenty miles an hour, while the ordinary gasoline car can be made to go two, three, or even four times as fast.

CHAPTER 13

IN THE CITY OF AUTOMOBILES

This morning we are in Detroit, the city of automobiles. The last lap of our long journey in big motor busses has brought us to the very door of our hotel. It seems to us that most of the big buildings of Detroit are automobile factories or factories that make parts used in motor cars. One of the tall skyscrapers in the city belongs to a great automobile company. In or near Detroit there are more than fifty automobile factories. And from this city come more than half of all the automobiles built each year in all the world.

Soon after breakfast Mary's

How different are cars to-day

Uncle Paul comes to our hotel for us. He is an official of one of the most important automobile companies here in Detroit. He is to take us out to his factory to see an automobile built.

"We want to find out everything about automobiles," Mary says to her uncle as we go to the front door where a number of cars await us.

"That's a big task," says her Uncle Paul laughing. "To find out everything about automobiles you should begin with the mines down under the earth. You should go to the gold mines, to the platinum mines, and to the mines where we get diamonds, for all of these things are needed to make the fine tools we use. You should go to the iron mines and the steel mills, and you should find out about zinc, copper, and tin. You should visit the oil wells and the chemical factories. You should not forget the cotton fields of the South nor the lands which send us jute. You should know, too, all about leather, lumber, and glass. Every one of these materials is used in making automobiles."

We tell Mary's uncle that we have already found out about all of these materials in our other Journey Club travels.

"Splendid!" he cries. "Then you can see the rest right here in Detroit. In our factories we will show you how the automobile maker waves his magic wand and turns these raw materials into a finished automobile ready to run."

Modern Magic

It seems indeed as though some one must have a powerful magic wand here at this automobile plant. Before our very eyes,

A factory where automobiles are made

The Journey Club travels by automobile [Bob, Mary, Helen, Edith, Dick, and Jack]

thousands of automobiles are rising out of the masses of iron, steel, and wood. This is modern magic. Its secret power lies in wonderful machines and the untiring work of the thousands of men and women who guide the raw materials through them.

"Why, it's like a small city," Edith exclaimed as our cars stopped at the factory gate. Instead of one great factory as we had expected, this company has more than forty. Its handsome brick and steel buildings cover many acres, and here and there tall chimneys pour out their black smoke into the sky. As we go from one factory to another, we walk along streets and sidewalks as fine and broad as those of a real city.

We follow our guide from one plant to another, stopping long enough in each to see just how the work is done. The designing and drafting rooms with their high tables and their drawings remind us of those in the locomotive works we visited. In the automobile factory, too, we see models of metal and wood made to guide the men who shape the different parts of the cars.

One factory turns out nothing but tools, and another plant is given over to re-making the steel that comes from the steel mills. The steel is cooked and cooled again and again until it has just the right hardness and strength.

As we walk along with our guide, he tells us that each automobile is made in two separate parts. He says the frame and the running gear are together called the *chassis* (sha'see), while the little house in which we sit when we ride is the automobile *body*. The chassis and the automobile body are built in different sections of this little city of factories.

The Making of an Automobile

"There are hundreds of parts, both large and small, in one automobile," Mary's uncle explains. "And most of them are made right here in our own factories." He takes us into one plant where the engines are put together. In another we see machines turning out axles, and we go through a third in which three hundred and fifty of the smaller parts are made. In one shop, great machines are cutting huge sheets

Great machines stamp out the steel parts

of metal into the shapes needed for the sides of the car, for its fenders and radiator covers and for other parts. These machines work like giant cooky-cutters. The sharp edges of their dies seem to bite through the hard metal as easily as our mothers' cake-cutters go through soft dough. One shop is filled with rows of ovens. Here certain parts are given a baking after they have had their baths of paint or enamel.

"This is a body plant," Uncle Paul says, as we enter another huge building of brick. "As the wood and the steel, the iron and the other materials go through the hands of these workmen here, our magic turns them into beautiful bodies for every kind of car. We have many experts who spend all their time planning to make our automobile bodies stronger and stronger, and more and more comfortable. Each year we try to make our models more beautiful."

The bodies are being put together

We like to watch the painting of these automobile bodies. We stand for a few moments beside men at work spraying their sides with streams of fine sand. As the millions of tiny grains are dashed against the metal, they clean it and scour it and make it ready for its first coat of paint.

Over there some men are spraying paint on a body for a large touring car. The paint comes out of the little nozzle in a fine mist like that of a lawn sprinkling hose. They tell us this way of painting is far better than using a brush. It is much quicker and the paint spreads on the metal more evenly. They show us how an endless chain pulls the painted car through a vast oven so that its paint may be baked on. When it comes out of the other end, more men turn their paint sprays upon it. This happens several times until at last the painted body is ready for polishing.

In still another shop we see the cushions and springs and the other fittings put in their places in the car's body. This shop is called the *Trim Shop*. This is perhaps because it is here that the bodies are given the trimmings that make them so beautiful and so comfortable.

Putting a Car Together

Most interesting to us of this whole city of factories are those where we see the different parts put together into a car. Each chassis frame is mounted on a truck. As it moves down the line past busy workmen, each one gives it some of its parts. Our guide calls this "the assembly line." We see the frames picking

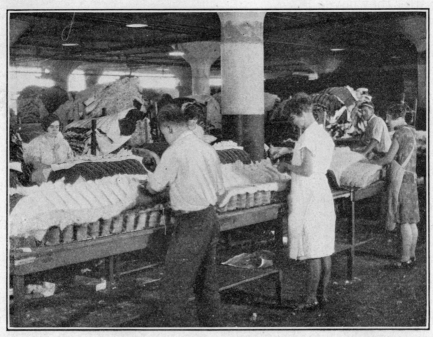

In one room the cushions are made

The body is finished

up their motors, their steering gears and their springs, their gasoline tanks and their rubber-tired wheels. We watch busy men putting on running boards, motor covers, and radiators. Here is a chassis all finished and ready to run.

"Oh, look up there," Mary exclaims. The chassis has stopped directly under a yawning hole in the ceiling above it. As we gaze upward, we see that an automobile body is being lowered through the wide opening in the floor overhead. It is dropped into its place upon the chassis, and as soon as its headlights and its windshield and its dashboard fittings are put on, it is ready to be tested. Uncle Paul says that an automobile chassis will fit several kinds of bodies. An automobile can often change bodies much as we change our hats.

"Where will that car go now?" Mary asks her Uncle Paul.

"It will perhaps have a short rest in our warehouse before it is shipped. But it will not stay there long. We have usually more orders than we can fill and within a day or two this car will be shipped off to a dealer in another part of the country. Perhaps this car will be driven away from our factory by some one who wishes to take it himself over the road, but more likely it will be sent to its buyer by freight. As we go out, I will show you our railroad yards. We have an electric crane for loading our automobiles, and our freight cars have special racks on their floors to hold the wheels of the cars so that they will not budge during their trips."

At the Automobile Show

Our way home takes us through a city where an automobile show is being held. We stop over a night so that we may spend a morning looking at the different cars on view there. A neat sign over each group of automobiles tells us just where they were made. Almost every one of our important automobile companies has a display on the floor of the great building in which the show is taking place. Some of these cars have even come

The bodies are let down through the ceiling

across the water from factories in Europe.

How many different kinds of automobiles there are! There are small cars and large cars and medium-sized cars. There are cheap cars and cars that cost a moderate amount. And then there are some that are very expensive. One of the finest of these last brings as much as ten or twelve smaller cars. How pretty the colors are this year! Reds, blues, and yellows, greens, browns, and grays, all shades and hues are to be seen in the shining paints that have been used to give these cars their gay dresses.

As we walk about, we see that each company makes several models. There are light open roadsters with just room for two persons. There are closed coupés and long, low touring cars. There are special models for taxicabs and sight-seeing busses, and elegant town cars for the fashionable folk who have chauffeurs in fine uniforms to drive them about. We see roomy sedans that will comfortably seat five and seven persons, and limousines with glass partitions that shut off the seats of the drivers from those of the passengers.

"What is that crowd over there?" Bob inquires of one of the men in charge of an exhibit.

At last the cars are loaded into trains

"You had best go and see," he replies with a smile. As we come near the crowd, we hear sounds of laughter. We make our way closer, and we too begin to laugh. "Oh, dear! Oh, dear!" Helen bends almost double with mirth. "Did you ever see anything one half so funny?" Before us stands one of the earliest automobiles. It looks like an old-fashioned buggy. On its

There are beautiful cars at the automobile show

seat perched so high up in the air are two people dressed in motoring costumes of over twenty years ago. How comical they look in their linen dusters and goggles! The woman has a long veil tied over her hat. She is holding tight to the side of her seat, for she is pretending to be afraid of this horseless carriage of hers. We wonder why they wore such curious clothes. Then a woman standing beside us remarks, "I remember I dressed just like that for my very first auto ride. And I was glad of my veil too, for we had no windshield to protect us. The dust flew all over our clothes and our faces."

We smile as we think of the difference between this clumsy carriage and our modern cars with their long beautiful bodies and their comfortable seats.

The Hard-Working Truck

Edith is specially interested in the lower-priced cars. She says that many of the farmers in her neighborhood have them. She asks us to stop in front of some of the booths where trucks are on show. We see small delivery trucks like those used by our stores at home, and by the farmers who bring vegetables in to our markets. There are other trucks with tremendous double wheels. These are specially made for hauling coal and heavy materials. The speaker in this booth tells us that a big truck can go from two hundred to three hundred miles in a day, while horses and wagons do well if they cover twenty miles in the same time. He says it costs twice as much to deliver a package with a horse and wagon as with an automobile.

One of the biggest of the trucks at this automobile show has been made for a railroad. We find out that many of our great railways use motor trucks as well as their steam and electric trains. Some have motor busses to carry passengers for short trips. Others use motor trucks to take small lots of freight to places near by. And, on lines where the stops are many, some railroads run gasoline passenger coaches over their rails.

"Look at the little house upon wheels," Mary exclaims. She calls us to see a bungalow car. It has been designed especially for campers. It has beds and a

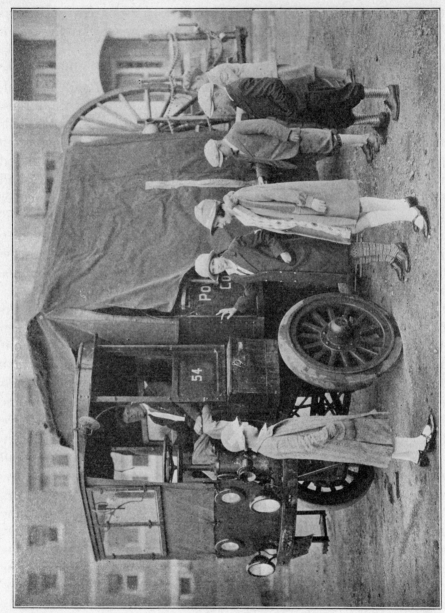

The Journey Club inspects a truck run by electricity [Edith, Mary, Helen, Dick, Jack, and Bob]

stove, electric lights, and even plumbing. We should like to tour in a car like this ourselves. What fun we could have eating our meals on its little table and sleeping on its folding beds at night!

Several of the other exhibits show camping outfits for an automobile. So many of our people go camping and touring that most cities and towns have set aside special camping grounds where they may spend the night.

Streams of motor gypsies flow over our highways at all times of the year. Like birds, they go south in the winter and to the resorts of the North when the hot weather comes. Many lovers of automobile touring have made the motor trip from one end of our land to the other, and last year enough motorists visited our national forests to fill a city half again as big as New York.

Some one was careless

Safety First

As we go out of the building a man at the door hands us a booklet with many pictures in it. Some of these we shudder to look at, for they show pictures of automobile accidents in which some one has been hurt. Last year there were in the world nearly a million people killed or injured by automobiles. This booklet says that in almost every case the accident need not have happened. Some one was careless and did not keep his eyes open. Drivers of automobiles have strict rules which they should obey. They should put out their hands when they wish to slow down or turn a corner. *They should not go too fast.* They should obey all traffic signals. But many times they do not. If we are to be safe as we cross the streets, we must be on guard every minute. We must take no chances.

There are rules for those of us who walk, too. The police are not so strict with those on foot as with those who drive cars. They count upon us to take care of ourselves. They expect us to keep to the sidewalks and the corner crossings. Rules for walkers are printed on the last page of our Safety First Booklets. Some of them read:

Look both ways when you cross a street.
Do not cross in the middle of a block or square.
Cross only at corners.
Do not play in crowded streets.
Do not get out of your automobile on the street side.

CHAPTER 14

GOOD ROADS

" If any town would make itself   If any town its own abodes
  The center of the map,   Of poverty would rid,
  Where folks will come and settle down   Let it go out and build good roads
  And live in plenty's lap;   Just as old Cæsar did."
                                              — OHIO MOTORIST.

Sally and Tom live in the country. Their father's farm is ten miles out of town on a rough dirt road. All through the bad winter weather this road is covered with snow or slush so deep that their light automobile cannot get through. Indeed, much of the time their horses can hardly pull the wagon over its ruts. When the spring comes with its warm sun, the frozen ground thaws. But their road then becomes worse than ever. There are many deep holes and soft marshy places. Their automobile gets stuck in the mud at every turn of the road.

Day in and day out Sally and Tom must stay near their home. Their school is too far away for them to walk to it, and except in the summer time when the road is dry, they rarely

Standard Highway Markings for All States
(Adopted by Joint Board of Interstate Highways)

163

Sally and Tom live on a poor road

go far away from their farm. They do not have much fun. Their father cannot seem to make his farm pay, no matter how hard he works. His buildings need painting. His fences want mending. His farm is run down. He has not the money to keep it up because with such a road he cannot take his crops to the market at the right time to get the best prices. Also, he cannot go back and forth easily to town to buy the supplies he should have for his farm work.

Betty and Peter live in the same state as Sally and Tom. But their life is quite different. Past their farm runs a smooth highway. No matter what the weather may be, the district school bus can come to their gate every day for them. In their automobile they go into town whenever there is an errand to do. On Saturday afternoons they can drive in to see the moving pictures and each Sunday morning they can ride to their church. They can visit their neighbors whenever they like. They go about their work and their play without any thought of the weather. They have quite as good a time as we who live in the city.

The home of this second family is a fine farmhouse with neat barns and other buildings. The father's motor truck carries his farm products to market at the time when he can get good prices for them. He does not have to wait for his road to dry to haul his supplies. When the snow comes, motor plows push the drifts off to the side of the road. He makes his farm pay and he keeps it in good order. He owes much to the smooth road that runs by his farm gate. A farm on a good road is always worth more.

The difference in the lives of these two families tells us the story of good roads. It shows plainly why we all want good roads in our neighborhood and why in our United States more than one billion dollars is being spent every year to turn roads like that of Sally and Tom into

Betty and Peter live on a good road

Where Betty and Peter go to school

Roads of Long, Long Ago

Among the very first road builders were the old Romans. Because they built long roads out from the city of Rome to every corner of the Roman Empire, there was a saying that "All roads lead to Rome!" These roads were made of blocks of hard stone. They were laid so well that now, nearly two thousand years later, some of them are still to be seen. The Roman roads were well planned. The heavy carts rattled their rough

smooth highways like the one that passes the gate of the farm where Betty and Peter live.

Sally's father cannot get to town in bad weather

Over good roads Betty's father takes his crops to market

wheels over a broad highway whose stone was often four feet in thickness. At each side of this there was a path of soft dirt along which the donkeys trudged with their burdens. These roads would cost enormous amounts to build to-day. Then they were built by Roman prisoners of war who received no wages.

Helen has brought to our meeting a verse written by a poet named McGroarty. It tells of English roads of long ago.

" All in the golden weather,
    Forth let us ride to-day,
    You and I together,
    On the King's Highway."

We think that sounds splendid. We picture the King's Highway as a broad shining road that wound its way through neat hedge-rows and green fields. But really the King's Highway was usually only a wide path or a rough dirt road. The lumbering coaches that passed over it were often up to their hubs in its mud and its mire.

It is the same with our old favorite, London Bridge. This singing game which we have played since we were tiny children was really written about a crude bridge of wood that stretched

London Bridge

far across the river Thames, at London. London Bridge took the place of a long-used ferry, and the "fair lady" of the song is thought by some people to have been the beautiful daughter of the old ferry-man.

> " London Bridge is falling down,
> Falling down, falling down.
> London Bridge is falling down,
> My fair lady."

From the Days of George Washington

In our Journey Club meeting to find out about how Patience True and John Adams traveled, we talked about the roads of Colonial days here in America. We spoke of the forest trails of the Indians and of the narrow post roads made by the colonists. Some of the best roads they built were of logs. Where the way was likely to be muddy, they laid down slender tree trunks, and then placed crosswise upon these many straight poles about ten or twelve feet in length. The cross poles lay close together like the ridges in Bob's corduroy trousers. That is probably the reason such roads were called corduroy roads.

Bob tells us again of the highways of our land when George Washington was President.

"As soon as the towns of the seacoast became crowded," he says, "our forefathers began to push into the West. They then found out how much they needed good roads. But the pioneers were poor. And roads and bridges cost much money. However, the young Government did build one or two roads that led into the unknown land back from the shores of the ocean. The first public highway was called the National Road. Over it many of the early pioneers went from the east into Ohio and later on into Indiana. Now this same road is a fine highway that crosses our land from New York to Los Angeles. Over the old

A good road of long ago

National Road passed stagecoaches with their teams of two and four horses, covered wagons with families bound for new homes in the West, and now and again a dashing one-horse chaise. Along its routes were many picturesque taverns where the travelers could rest or get food and drink.

There were no real highways like the ones we motor over to-day until many, many years after George Washington died. For a long time, the best roads of our land were made and run by private companies. To get their money to build and keep up the roads, these companies

A toll gate

required that every one who traveled upon them pay a tax. This tax was called a *toll*. Toll houses were built every so often. These had long poles which the gate-keepers let down to bar the road until the travelers had paid. Such poles were also called pikes. They turned back those who would not pay. So the roads were known as "turnpikes" or often simply as "pikes."

It was over a road like these that General Phil Sheridan rode on his famous twenty mile ride during our Civil War. One verse of a poem about him reads:

" But there is a road from Winchester
    town,
  A good, broad highway leading down;
  And there, through the flush of the
    morning light,
  A steed as black as the steeds of night
  Was seen to pass as with eagle flight."

— T. B. READ.

Roads of To-day

Paolo is one of our Journey Club members who until lately

A dirt road

lived across the Atlantic Ocean in Europe. He says Europe has some of the best roads in the world. He tells us the French boast that a traveler can walk from one end of France to the other without wetting his feet. French roads are indeed good, as are also those of Switzerland, Germany, and other countries in Europe. These countries are all far older than the United States. Their land is smaller and more crowded than ours and their paved roads often reach more of their people. In many of these countries the government has full charge of all the highways. It employs trained engineers to build them and to keep them in the very finest condition.

Wouldn't John Adams be surprised if he could come back to earth and go with the Journey Club for a ride in a swift automobile over the smooth hard roads that lead out from our city? How his eyes would pop at these broad highways winding up hill and down dale, through towns,

The same road covered with gravel

The Journey Club watches a steam shovel [Mary, Edith, Helen, Jack, Bob, and Dick]

villages, and cities! We should have to tell him, however, that it was not until the bicycle and the automobile were invented that we had any roads so smooth as these. Before then our people depended on wagons and carriages, and they were often content with uneven dirt roads.

Edith says the country roads of the past had little ridges running across them to turn the rain water into ditches dug along the sides of the roads. Country folk used to call such ridges "Thank-you-ma'ams." They always slowed down their horses when they came to a Thank-you-ma'am, for if they tried to go over it too quickly they were liable to be jolted out of their seats.

With the coming of the bicycle and the automobile, every one wanted to ride farther and farther into the country. These vehicles went so much faster than the old horse and buggy that good smooth roads were almost a necessity. Each year more and more people interested themselves in the good roads movement. Highway Departments were formed in most of our states, and

little by little our splendid system of roads is being built up.

Dick's father has given us for our Museum a map that shows

Good roads are level

the principal highways of the United States. It looks like a checkerboard. The roads run east and west, and north and south through one state after another. They are "through" roads. They make a criss-cross network all over our land. There seem to be more roads in the central and eastern parts of our country than in the West. That is because there are more people living in the East, and more factories and

Steam shovels level the earth

There are to-day in our land enough roads to stretch all the way round the world more than a hundred and twenty times. And yet our road-building is only begun. Our land is so vast and it grows so fast that our road-builders cannot keep up with the people who go to live in its new and far-away places. Every state is doing its very best and

mills whose goods must be hauled from one place to another.

Most of these "through" roads were paid for half by the Government and half by the states through which they run. Other roads here in our own State were built by our State, or by our County and State working together. A few of our local roads were built by our County.

our Government at Washington has a special Bureau of Public

Rolling the roadbed

Roads. Its men spend all their time helping our states to give us better highways.

Building a Road

Put on your hats and coats! For the last part of our Good Roads meeting we are to ride out into the country to see a new road being built. Automobiles take us flying along over the broad streets of our city. We stop for a few minutes at one place where a new street is being cut through.

We watch the huge steam shovel gnawing the unwanted dirt out of the roadway and spitting it into trucks that will carry it off.

The man in charge tells us that the very first thing in building either a street or a road is to lay out the way it is to go. Next, its route must be made as straight and as level as possible. In the country steam shovels like this are used to cut away whole hillsides, or to eat pathways through them. Other machines drill holes

Pouring the concrete

so that charges of dynamite may blast tunnels through the mountains where they cannot be cut

Concrete really makes roads of molded stone

and shrubs and they often trim away branches so that a fine view may be seen. In France the Government plants rows of shade trees along each side of its roads. Beside our great highways, too, more and more trees are being planted every year.

Now we have reached the country road we are seeking. We park our cars and walk along to where the road-builders are working. They explain how the tops of hills have been cut away and hauled to fill in the low places, and how ditches were dug along the sides of the road. Some of the earth has been scraped from the sides to the center and leveled off on the top by a road-scraper. The finished road will slope gently to each side so that all water will run

away. Good road-makers always plan their roads without hairpin turns or hidden curves so as to make them safer. They also try to make them beautiful. They take care not to destroy flowers

off into the ditches. Here and there, where they were needed, pipes of iron, burnt clay, or concrete have been laid across under this road to help carry the rain water away. The dirt foundation has been pressed smooth by a giant road-roller and the road is now ready for its hard upper coating.

These men are building a concrete highway. That clumsy of this machine. Just enough water is added to mix these together into a soft workable mass. With a noisy clatter, the machine churns the mixture about until it flows out as concrete that

Smoothing a dirt road

machine standing there on the roadbed is a huge concrete mixer. It reminds us of the one we saw in our trips to find out about houses built of concrete blocks. Sand, fine broken rock, and a grayish powder called Portland cement are poured in at one end spreads over the road. In some places this concrete mixing is done at a central point and the wet concrete is hauled in motor trucks, which dump it out on the roadbed. We see that rails of metal have been set up along this roadway to keep the wet concrete mixture in place. Following the path of the spreader, comes another machine which smooths the top of the wet mass of concrete We sprinkle this with water so that it will protect the concrete from the sun until it is hard. In some places we use a damp cloth,

Laying an asphalt road

until it is as even as the floor of your house.

"We often make our roads stronger by laying slender steel rods in the concrete," the road-builder says. "These keep the concrete from cracking. They make it last longer. When the concrete has been spread and set and the road is finished we cover it with a coating of earth or straw. called burlap, to cover our concrete, or we spray it with a certain chemical mixture. This chemical keeps it moist while it is hardening."

When dry, concrete is almost as hard as stone. It is really molded stone. It makes one of the best highways, and the heaviest kind of hauling can be done upon it with safety.

What Roads Are Made Of

The road-builder tells us of many different kinds of roads. He speaks of dirt roads with their ruts and the mud holes that come in wet weather. He says roads of gravel or of sand and clay mixed together dry off very quickly. They are far better than dirt roads, for they do not hold water. These roads are carefully graded and sloped. The earth from the sides is scraped up toward the center into a crown so that the water will run off. Drains are put in and the road is rolled until it is hard and smooth.

We hear, too, of roads made of blocks of stone. These last a long, long time. But they are the most expensive, and they are hard on the trucks and the cars that drive over them. Roads or streets of stone blocks are often disliked, too, because they are so noisy and bumpy. There

are very few except in some of our cities.

"Two roads that wear well," the road-man goes on, "are asphalt and macadam. Asphalt

Rolling a macadam road

is a black sticky stuff that is found under the ground or in lakes in certain lands. Natural asphalt is hard to get, so we make most of what we use from

Some asphalt is gotten from lakes

the first to think of building roads in this way. The first layer of rock is crushed into pieces about as big as your fist. This is pressed down with a heavy road-roller, and then comes another layer of stones about the size of a walnut. This too is rolled, and then the top coating of fine chips of rock and rock dust is put on. When the water is sprinkled upon this and heavy road-rollers have been passed over it, the rock dust and the water form a kind of cement that fills in the spaces between the small stones. Sometimes a special cement of asphalt or tar is used in such rock-layer roads."

crude petroleum. Coal tar is used often in the same way as asphalt. Asphalt has helped to make streets for hundreds of years. There are probably a number of asphalt streets in your own city. Most of those we ride on to-day are built with a foundation of concrete like that we are laying here. A layer of finely crushed stone mixed with asphalt is put down upon the concrete to form the surface of the street. Heavy road-rollers go over this again and again until it is smooth.

"Macadam roads have upon them layers of crushed rock that have been sprinkled and rolled until they form a solid mass. They are called macadam because a Scotchman of that name was

Macadam is many layers of rock

As we stand watching the concrete being spread on the highway, we are told of other roads which are made of brick and wood blocks. A brick road is almost as lasting as stone. Road bricks are especially hard. They are usually laid in sand on a base of concrete and the cracks are filled with a tar-like stuff. During our

Some roads are made of brick

travels we have ridden upon streets made of wood blocks that have been dipped in a hot oil to make them water-tight. We remember how smoothly and silently our cars rolled along over them. Wooden roads are good in hospital neighborhoods, where quiet is wanted. Many of the streets of Paris are paved with wood.

There is a road on top of the Great Wall of China

We admire the beauty of our roads

Ewing Galloway

The road-builder tells us of strange roads in other lands. In India he says there are some highways covered with hard rubber, and in Valencia, Spain, a road made of steel has been in use for more than twenty years. We ourselves have traveled over all the others who own automobiles pay most of the bill," is the reply. "The Government at Washington, and your State, and your County all have a part in their building, but the money they use is what you have paid in taxes of one kind or other.

Roads must have bridges to cross the streams

highways built of oyster and clam shells. There are many shell roads in our states along the seashore. We tell the road-man how we once traveled over the broad highway of stone and earth on the top of the famous Great Wall of China.

Who Pays for Our Roads

"Who pays for all these roads of ours?" Jack asks the road-builder.

"Your fathers and mothers and

The roads belong to every one. That is why they are called public highways. Each automobile owner pays a tax when he gets his numbered license plate. In many states, too, the price of a gallon of gasoline is a few cents higher than the gas really costs. This is a gasoline tax. Those extra pennies go into the State's treasury. They help to build new roads and to repair the old ones.

Roads need constant repair

"You see," the road-builder explains, "although it costs a great deal to build roads in the first place, it costs also to keep them smooth after automobiles and heavy trucks have begun running upon them. When the first breaks and cracks come, they must be filled in at once or the road will soon be full of deep holes. The Chinese have an old proverb that 'A road is good for ten years and bad for ten thousand.' That is often true in China because they do not know how to repair their roads. Last year forty dollars were spent for each of the ninety-three thousand miles of snowy roads that we cleared. In all our states where much snow falls during the win-ter, motor snowplows are kept busy pushing away the drifts so that the automobiles and the trucks can make their way through."

As we ride back to our homes, Mary describes a trip over the Dixie Highway that goes from Chicago to Miami. We speak also of the great Lincoln Highway and other roads that cross our land from coast to coast or from our northernmost states to the states farthest south.

Roads must be cleared of snow

CHAPTER 15

SHIPS

A PAGEANT WRITTEN AND PRE-
SENTED BY

THE JOURNEY CLUB

CAST OF CHARACTERS

(In the order of their appearance)

Neptune, the Greek God of the Sea	PAOLO
Esther, a girl of Bible times	EDITH
Marcus, a Roman galley slave	DICK
Borghild, the Viking's daughter	HELEN
Christopher Columbus .	JACK
Patience True, a girl of Colonial America . .	MARY
Robert Fulton . . .	FRANK
John Ericsson	HARRY
Hetty, who lived on a canal boat . . .	NAN
A Member of the Jour- ney Club . . .	BOB

(The stage is the end of Mary's living room, across which curtains are hung. As the curtains open, a table is seen at the right.)

PROLOGUE: THE ANCIENT RULER OF THE SEA

(Enter Neptune clad in a loose sleeveless robe of water-green cloth that falls below his knees. In his right hand he holds a gilded trident. In his left he carries a dolphin made of painted cardboard. He stands straight and proud. His appearance suggests power and strength.)

Neptune speaks: Behold, Great Neptune, king of the seas! From my golden palace on the sandy bed of the ocean I rule the waters of the wide earth. The sea-creatures bow before me. The oceans, the rivers, the lakes, and the gushing springs of the mountains all obey my commands.

I send out my herald, young Triton, to blow a loud blast upon

185

his shell trumpet. And lo, a tempest arises that brings dread to all sailors. I bid him blow softly, and straightway the waves become smooth as a floor. I give the word, and the rivers and lakes

Early boat of skins

flow over the land in a terrible flood. In Greece the seamen build me fine temples where prayers are said for smooth seas. Well do they know that I am the master of all that ride on the waves. None may come safely over the sea save by my will. I have but to stir the billows and the ships crack like eggshells under the beat of my waves. No

ship built by man can withstand my forces. (*Neptune shakes his trident in the air, then exits.*)

Scene I: In Bible Times

(*Enter Esther, dressed in a loose gown of blue cotton. Her neck and arms are covered with strings of bright beads. In her ears are hoop rings of yellow gilt. She wears leather sandals laced round her bare ankles. In her hand she carries a miniature Noah's Ark.*)

Esther speaks: Esther is my name. I lived long ago in the times of the Bible. I have come back to earth to tell you of the very earliest ships and also of the boats used in Bible days. When the world was young, its first boats were made of hollowed-out logs. Then some one thought of putting a mast high over the boat with a hide stretched upon it to catch the force of the wind. With such rude wind-catchers small craft could be blown swiftly to and fro over the water. Later two paddles were used in the form of oars.

But it was not until men learned

to build boats of wooden planks and to seal their cracks with a tar-like pitch that real ships could be made. The Egyptians and a people called the Phœnicians, at the eastern end of the Mediterranean Sea, are thought to have been the world's first shipbuilders. Their wooden ships had many oars and they often used sails as well. Besides wooden ships they made curious boats of woven reeds, which they smeared with pitch to keep out the water. It was in a tiny basketwork boat of this kind that the Egyptian Princess found the baby Moses floating on the River Nile so many thousand years ago.

The most famous boat in all the Bible was Noah's Ark. For those times the Ark was the biggest boat in the world. It was half as long as the largest ships on the ocean to-day. Its planks were of gopher wood and its cracks were sealed with an asphalt like that you put on your paved streets. Noah had no way to guide or move his Ark from one place to another. It floated hither and yon over the raging waters of the flood.

In those early days, seamen did not have compasses with which to steer their ships. They set their course by the sun, the moon, and the stars. When the mists covered these up, they drifted about until the skies became clear again.

An Egyptian ship

Vessels that went forth over the ocean were often gone for weeks and months at a time. Ships are spoken of in many places in the Bible. You may read of fishing boats, sailing ships, and trading vessels. In the Psalms of David are these verses:

"They that go down to the sea in ships,
    that do business in great waters:
These see the works of the Lord,
    and his wonders in the deep."

(*Esther bows and lays her model of the Ark on the end of the table at the right. Exit.*)

Scene II: A Roman Galley

(*Enter Marcus. He is dressed in a short sleeveless tunic of coarse*

A Roman galley

ragged cloth and worn sandals. His shoulders are bent. His face is sad. He carries a model of an old Roman galley with its three tiers of oars.)

Marcus speaks: I am Marcus, a poor galley slave. My lot was a hard one. For many years I served long hours on one of the terrible galleys of the Roman navy. Our galley was large. There were three tiers of oarsmen, each tier sitting above the other. More than two hundred and fifty of us slaves were chained to our places on the rowers' benches and often four of us bent to wield one oar. On the deck above, the timekeeper set our pace with the beats of his mallet. Thump! Thump! Thump! Thump! Row! Row! Row! Row! In time with the thumping we swung our oars. If one of us lagged — swish, down on our bare backs came the slave driver's whiplash.

Swiftly we sent the war galley speeding over the water. There were sails, too, but the greatest speed came from the sweat of our backs. The Greeks and other neighboring nations had war galleys like ours. The

Early merchant vessels

merchant vessels of those days often went under sail only. They were not in a hurry and they could wait for the winds. They needed the rowers' space inside the ship for their cargoes of grain.

(*Marcus lays his model of a Roman galley beside Esther's Ark, gives a salute, and exits.*)

SCENE III: THE SEA ROVERS

(*Enter Borghild, dressed in the costume of her Viking fathers. She wears a blouse of silver to represent a coat of mail, and a full skirt that comes to her knees. A loose cape is knotted around her shoulders. Her feet are shod with high boots laced over long socks of wool. On her head is a metal helmet with curving horns at each side. In one hand she bears a round metal shield and in the other a model of a Viking ship. She stands straight and free, head up and chest high.*)

Borghild speaks: I am Borghild, daughter of the Vikings, the Northmen of old. From their homes in Denmark, Norway, and Sweden, my forefathers set forth over the cold northern seas in their pirate ships. During each summer these Norse sea-rovers brought terror to the people on the coasts of France and England, for they came down upon them in hordes and plundered their towns. Later they came to conquer and to settle.

A viking ship

The part of France that to-day is called Normandy gets its name from these Norsemen.

The Viking sea rovers were brave and strong. They feared neither foe nor Neptune's tempest. Some of them, under the daring Leif Ericson, are thought to have crossed the Atlantic Ocean to America five hundred years before Columbus came.

(*Borghild walks with dignity to the table, where she lays down her model of a Viking ship. Raising her right hand in the Norse salute, she turns and exits.*)

SCENE IV: COLUM-
BUS CROSSES THE
OCEAN

(*Enter Christopher
Columbus, dressed
like the picture of the
great explorer in our
history books. His
model is that of his
ship, the Santa
Maria.*)

Columbus speaks:
I, Christopher Co-
lumbus, have come to tell of the
greatest sea voyage of all history.
With my little sailing vessel, the
Santa Maria, and with her two

Christopher Columbus

sister ships, the *Niña*
and the *Pinta*, I
set forth from Spain
across the vast ocean.
For long journeys
over the raging deep,
oars would not have
been of much help.
We had to depend
upon our sails to
carry us over that
Sea of Darkness. I
lived in the age of
sails. My ships were
small. The *Santa Maria* was but
eighty feet long and twenty-five
feet wide. We dreaded Old Neptune's tempests in fear that our
masts and our sails might be carried away and that our wooden
ships might be dashed into pieces.
Many times my sailors wished to
turn back, and it took all my force
to keep them at their task. At
last, on the seventieth day of our
journey, the unknown shores
came into sight. So was the
New World of America dis-
covered. This poem tells a part
of the story of my great voyage:

Behind him lay the gray Azores,
Behind the Gates of Hercules;
Before him not the ghost of shores;
Before him only shoreless seas.

The *Santa Maria*

A ship of the Fourteenth Century

The good mate said: "Now must we
    pray,
For lo! the very stars are gone.
Brave Admiral, speak; what shall I
    say?"
"Why say, 'Sail on! sail on! and
    on!'"

             — JOAQUIN MILLER

Many were the explorers who
followed me over the sea. They
sailed to South America, and
around the Cape of Good Hope.
I myself made four journeys to
the New World and my success
did much to encourage the building of better ships. Others wished
to share in the riches of the land
I had found and my ships were
only the first of the unending procession of vessels that were blown
by the winds across to America.

*(The model of Columbus' ship is
placed next in line before he exits.)*

SCENE V: THE GOOD SHIP
MAYFLOWER

*(Patience True enters, dressed in
the costume of a Pilgrim girl. She
holds before her the model of the
Mayflower.)*

Patience True speaks: Before
your eyes is a model of the Good
Ship *Mayflower*. In the year
1620 it brought us and our Pilgrim
friends safely over the stormy
Atlantic to our new home in
America. What a voyage we
had! The *Speedwell*, the other
ship that started out with us, had
to turn back, and it took us sixty-
three days to force our way

A warship of the Sixteenth Century

through the waves to Plymouth Rock.

The *Mayflower* was of wood, just like the ship of Columbus. Like his vessel, too, it was the wind in our sails that brought us first and few horses to carry us over the Indian trails. The easiest way to go from one place to another was in a boat of some kind. I have already told the Journey Club how our friends

The Good Ship *Mayflower*

to port. But our ship was almost twice the size of the little *Santa Maria* and it carried one hundred and two men, women, and children.

In the days when I lived on the shores of New England, every one wanted his home beside a river or lake. There were no roads at traveled in dugouts, in canoes, and on rafts, and how we were ferried over the rivers. Little by little our men made bigger and better boats and at last our ship carpenters began to turn out ships as fine and as seaworthy as the *Mayflower*. Sailing ships from England and other countries of

Europe brought us the things we could not make for ourselves. But best of all they brought over more and more brave people who were willing to work to carve their homes out of the wilderness of the New World.

Most of our boats were for fishing or trading between our settlements. Every well-to-do family had its own boat tied fast to its landing just as families to-day have their automobiles standing ready for use in their garages.

(*She places her model on the table and exits.*)

SCENE VI: THE FIRST STEAM-BOAT

(*Robert Fulton appears. He is clad in a close-fitting suit of dark cloth and his neck is bound round with an old-fashioned stock. He brings with him a model of his first steamship.*)

Robert Fulton speaks: Robert Fulton stands before you. I was born almost one hundred and fifty years after Patience True came to America in the Good Ship *Mayflower.* When I was a boy, the rivers of our land were still

A statue of Robert Fulton

the main streets of our nation. All kinds of boats went back and forth upon them, trading between the towns on the banks or carrying new settlers to the lands farther west.

There were wide-bottomed skiffs moved along by oars. There were keel boats with sails, and barges and lumbering arks with steering oars so heavy that it took two men to wield them. One of the best boats of my boyhood was the flatboat. Some flatboats had a roof and sides like a house. Whole families traveled upon them. Pens for the animals were placed at one end

sink. Several inventors here in America made steamboats that would run after a fashion. But people did not become truly interested until I built the *Clermont*, the first real steamboat. Its steam engine was joined to

A flatboat on the Mississippi

and play yards for the children were built on the roofs.

All these early wooden boats were clumsy. They went very slowly. Over in England and France, steam engines were already in use for pumping water out of mines. Many men tried to think out a way to put steam to work in moving boats, too. It was hard to build a steam engine that was not so heavy that it would make the boat

paddle wheels on the sides of the boat that sent it through the water surely and steadily.

How exciting my trial trip was on that day in 1807 when my boat steamed along on the Hudson River! Every one gaped with wonder at a boat that would move without oars or sails. My boat went only about five miles an hour. But as soon as it was found that paddle wheels and steam engines could work so well together, steamboats were built that would go much faster.

At first steamboats were small. They ran on the rivers, little by little taking the place of the old sailing packets that had long carried passengers from one settlement to another. A man named Lewis Pease wrote this verse about them.

The *Clermont*

" A fig for all your clumsy craft,
   Your pleasure boats and packets,
The steamboat lands you safe and
   soon
   At Mansfield's, Trott's, or Bracket's."

I did not live to see the first steamship cross the Atlantic Ocean. The steamship *Savannah* that went from Georgia to Liverpool traveled part of the way by her own steam and her paddle wheels. Though her fuel gave out and she had to use sails for a part of the voyage, she proved that a steamboat could cross the ocean. The little ship *Sirius* was the first to go all the way across the sea by steam.

(*With a courtly bow, Robert Fulton exits, having left his ship model behind him.*)

SCENE VII: SHIPS OF IRON AND STEEL

(*John Ericsson, who enters next, is dressed in dark clothes with a sea captain's cap and cape. In one hand he carries a model of a screw propeller, and in the*

The *Savannah*

other a clipper ship. He has in his pocket a large picture of the Monitor.

John Ericsson speaks: When Robert Fulton died, I was a boy twelve years of age living in

"Old Ironsides"

Sweden. By the time I was grown, the rivers were filled with puffing steamboats. Some were used, too, for crossing the ocean. Yet sailing ships were still the kings of the sea. The finest of all were the graceful clipper ships made in Baltimore and in the shipyards of New England. These slim, sharp-prowed vessels carried many sails. They went at great speed across the ocean waves, and

often they beat the vessels with steam paddles. Clipper ships were used for trading with China and the Far East. Many sailed, too, around Cape Horn to California, where gold had just been discovered. One of the fastest crossings to Ireland made by the clipper ships was twelve days. American sailing ships at that time were the finest and fastest in all the world.

As steamships were made better and better, clipper ships lost their lead. I, John Ericsson, helped to drive them off the sea with my invention of this screw propellor. I was the first to think of a way to have a great screw like this turned swiftly round and round by the steam engines in such a way that it would push the ship ahead through the water. It was soon found that a screw was both faster and stronger than Fulton's paddle wheel, which often was broken by the stormy seas. Since my discovery most new steamboats have been built with one, two, and even three or four screws. (*He lays his propellor and the clipper down on the table.*)

(*Enter Hetty. She is dressed simply in a red gingham dress and she is barefoot and bareheaded.*

The *Merrimac* and the *Monitor* in a famous battle

But it is as the inventor of the *Monitor* that most people remember me. (*He unrolls a picture of this famous ship.*) She was the first iron-clad vessel ever used in our navy and in some ways the forefather of all the steel-clad battleships in the world to-day.

(*John Ericsson hangs his picture over the table as he exits.*)

The model she brings is of a canal boat.)

Hetty speaks: I lived all my life upon a canal boat. It was my only home. Early in the history of America, canals were dug to join one body of water with another. In this way people could travel in boats for great distances. George Washington was one of the very first to see

A canal boat of early days

how much good canals could do our new country.

A canal is really a broad ditch filled with water. It is dug through the ground deep enough to allow a flat-bottomed boat like this to float upon its surface. (*Hetty holds out her model of a canal boat.*) I loved our life on the canal boat. I could sit in

Hetty lives on a canal boat

the sun on the top of the house in the center of the boat and watch the mules that pulled us slowly along. They trudged steadily over a path at the side of the canal, towing our boat by means of the rope to which they were hitched. My brother Jerry and I would take turns in walking along the tow-path with the mules to keep them at their task. Grover Cleveland and James Garfield, both Presidents of the United States, trod the tow-path when they were boys.

To-day there are several thousand miles of canals in our United States. But only half of them are in use, and their boats now carry nothing but freight. For the railroad has taken away all the passengers of the canal boats, and much of their freight, too. Our first great canal was the Erie Canal that joined the Hudson River with Lake Erie at Buffalo. On its round-the-world trips the Journey Club has gone through the two most famous canals in the world. These are the Suez Canal that joins the Red Sea with

the Mediterranean, and the great Panama Canal that cuts through the Isthmus of Panama from the Atlantic to the Pacific.

(*Hetty lays down her model of a canal boat, waves her hand, and exits.*)

In a canal

SCENE IX. SHIPS OF TO-DAY

(*A Journey Club member enters dressed in his everyday clothes. He has a model of a modern river boat in one hand and of a great ocean liner in the other.*)

The Journey Club Member speaks: This is the kind of a river boat on which the Journey Club likes to travel. With their real beds and their running hot and cold water, the cabins on it are quite as comfortable as our

A ship passing through the Panama Canal

bedrooms at home. And its decks are broad enough for merry games of tag and I-spy.

This liner is a model of the giant ocean steamship upon which the Journey Club is to make its next trip. It is hundreds of times as big as Columbus' *Santa María*. With its great screws it plows its way swiftly over the sea whatever the weather. We shall be as comfortable upon it as though we were at home, and quite as safe. I have a little poem that tells how a Journey Club member feels when he goes for a trip over the ocean.

" I'm on the sea! I'm on the sea!
I am where I would ever be;
With the blue above, and the blue below,
And silence wheresoe'er I go;
If a storm should come and awake the deep,
What matter? I shall ride and sleep."
— BRYAN WALLER PROCTER

A modern ocean liner approaches New York

On board a river boat [Bob, Edith, Mary, Dick, Jack, and Helen]

(The last of the models are placed in line. The Journey Club Member exits.)

Epilogue. Neptune Conquered

(Enter Neptune dressed as before. But his bearing has changed. He droops like one beaten. His trident drags.)

Neptune speaks: "Woe is me! Woe is me! Behold my enemies lined up against me! (*He points to the line of ships.*) What can I do? My ancient power is gone. I send a storm, but to-day no sea captain falls to his knees and prays me for smooth weather. These ocean giants ride safely over my tempest waves. It is rare indeed that I can cause a shipwreck. To be sure, there was the great *Titanic* which I sank with an iceberg. But that will perhaps never happen again. Whether I will it or not, hundreds of thousands travel over my oceans with no thought of me. I may as well give up my trident to man, for he has conquered me now.

(He sadly lays his trident behind the ships on the table and exits.)

CHAPTER 16

ON A HUGE OCEAN STEAMSHIP

Dong! Dong! Dong! "All ashore that are going ashore." The deck boys pound out this warning on their brass gongs. People are hurrying this way and that, saying good-by to their friends, and looking after their baggage. Late-comers are running up the gangplank that leads from the dock on to the great ship. All is bustle and hubbub.

A sailing vessel

Automobiles brought the Journey Club to the dock in good time. We showed our tickets and our passports to the steamship officials and took care that our trunks and our bags were aboard. Now we are standing at the rail looking over the side of the vessel at the crowds below on the dock. Our own friends are waiting there to see us start forth on our journey over the ocean to Europe. Now the ship's siren blows forth its shrill warning. Orders are given. The gangplanks are drawn off. We feel the ship tremble ever so slightly as its engines whirr and its screws begin to move round.

"Good-by! Good-by!" We wave our caps and our handker-

Steamships in their docks

chiefs as long as we can make out the friends we are leaving behind us. Now the dock is out of sight. We are steaming down New York harbor towards the Statue of Liberty. We pass many ships. There are ocean liners from other lands. There are freighters from all parts of the world. We even see a few sailing vessels with masts and rigging. Only about one-half of the ships that come into New York harbor carry the American flag. Great Britain stands first among all the nations in her number of ships and the United States second with about half as many.

A Great Ocean Giant

This morning we are in mid-ocean. For three days we have been living in this floating hotel, making our way swiftly and surely across the wide seas. There is nothing in sight but the great dome of light blue sky over our heads and the dark blue waters rolling out on all sides to the horizon. Our ship is one of the largest afloat. It is so long that if it were set down in a city street it would cover almost two blocks and its top deck would reach higher than the roof of a ten-story office building. The deck-steward tells us that if we were to visit all parts of the vessel we should walk more than nine miles.

"What a lot of people there are on board," Mary says. "There must be almost a thousand."

"There are nearly five times that number," the deck-steward replies. "There are more than three thousand passengers, and eleven hundred officers, sailors, stewards, cooks, and others who serve the ship in some way."

Five thousand people! That is more than there are in many a small American city. Think of a whole city of men, women, and children riding over the waves inside a steel shell no thicker than two of your fingers! The genii of Aladdin's famous lamp built

Up the gangplank

Bob and Helen try on their life belts

nothing more wonderful than this ship of ours. During the World War, on one single trip, it

Our Days at Sea

We enjoy our days at sea. When we wake in the morning,

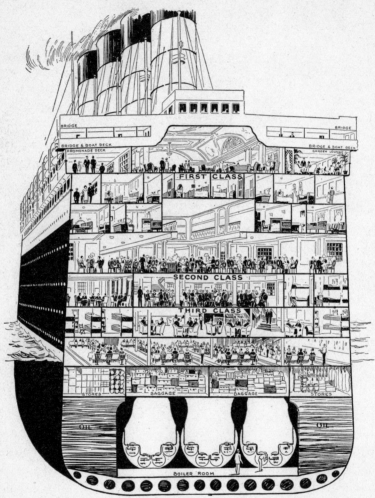

A cross section of our ship

carried more than eleven thousand soldiers safely over the Atlantic Ocean to France.

the fresh salt air is blowing in our portholes, as a ship's windows are called. Our staterooms are smaller but they are quite as comfortable as our bedrooms at home. We have drawers and closets into which to put our clothes, and we sleep in real beds. On some of our other sea trips, our beds were berths, built one over the other like those of a Pullman. Hot and cold fresh water flows from the faucets into our toilet basins when we wish to wash our faces, and each morning we splash about in the salt water of the baths not far down the hall. Some of the staterooms have their own private baths.

Everything in our rooms is screwed tight to the walls and the floors. In stormy weather our ship pitches and tosses and our suitcases dance a jig over the carpet.

We are always hungry at sea. In addition to our three regular meals we enjoy the mid-morning soup, and the tea and the sandwiches which the deck steward passes around at four o'clock. There are several dining rooms on our ship. There are tea rooms and a restaurant, a winter garden, and a main dining room with small tables covered with fine linen and shining silver.

A stateroom has regular beds

There are special dining rooms, too, for the smaller children.

The sea air is so brisk that we are full of life. Each fine morning we walk or run a mile around the broad decks, passing the rows of long steamer chairs where other passengers are sitting chatting or reading. Now and then we go for a dip in the salt water of the swimming pool and we spend much time in the play room and the gymnasium. every one off the ship in case of an accident, and in our cabins we have each a life belt which would keep us afloat if we should be shipwrecked.

There are beautiful dining rooms

But best of all, we like our games in the open air. On the top deck we play shuffle board and ring toss and a kind of ship tennis. Sometimes we jump rope and play hide and seek among the lifeboats. There are enough of these lifeboats to take On the top deck, too, are the traveling quarters for the pet dogs of the passengers. We like to visit the kennels with their great police dogs and their bright-eyed little terriers. Now and then the owners permit us to take the dogs for a run over the decks.

After lunch some of us get books from the ship's library and snuggle down in our deck chairs. Later we go in to see the moving pictures that are held each afternoon in one of the parlors. Or we may hear a concert played by the ship's orchestra. At night there are dances and entertainments for the older people. The parlors of this ship are splendid. Soft easy chairs, beautiful hangings, and fine carpets make them as grand as many a king's palace in olden times.

prow of our boat, cutting its way through the white-capped waves, that we can believe we are on a ship and not in a huge hotel at a summer resort.

Children have their own dining rooms

Although we are so far out here on the ocean, we can get word from our friends at home by means of the radio. Radio news from America and other parts of the world is printed in the ship's newspaper, and when we wish we can send wireless messages to our families. Indeed, it is only when we look at the

We Look over Our Ship

"Would you boys and girls like to go with me over our ship?" Mr. Roberts, the ship's purser, greets us with this question one morning when we come in to breakfast. Of course, we shout

"Yes, thank you." And when the meal is eaten we set forth with him down the long halls.

We already know about our own, the first class part of the ship. Mr. Roberts explains that there are three classes of passengers. He takes us through the plainer, and the passengers are somewhat more crowded. But still we think they must be very comfortable, too. They pay least of all for their passage.

"These are the kitchens and the storerooms," says Mr. Roberts. We go through one room

There is a great lounge

second class where the staterooms and parlors are not quite so fine as in the first class. The people who travel here pay a smaller fare than we. He shows us also through the third class. Here the rooms are still smaller and after another where white-capped men and boy cooks are busy at work at tables and stoves. We are several stories below our cabins and decks, down in the very heart of the vessel. We see in the kitchens huge steel kettles

A game of push ball on deck

that cook barrels of soup, broilers where one hundred lamb chops may sizzle side by side, and bake shops where bread and cake are baked by the bushels. Six thousand pounds of meat are cooked

the vegetables, the fruits, milk, and butter for feeding the five thousand persons aboard our ship.

In the Engine Room

Next, the elevators drop us down several stories further to the engine room, where we meet one of the ship's engineers. He explains how the great machines we see here turn the screw propellers in the water in such a way that their whirling blades send our floating palace ahead at a speed of twenty-five to thirty miles an hour. He says our ship can make the trip to England in less than six days.

Some people play shuffle board

here in one day and a barrel of flour is often used at a baking. In the store-rooms are enough supplies to fill several large food stores. There are thousands of dozens of eggs, tons of coffee and tea, and sugar, jam, and flour by the thousands of pounds. We shiver when the doors of the cold storage rooms open. Within their walls with their coverings of artificial snow, are kept the meat and

"Our ship burns oil," the Chief Engineer says. "In the past most steamships heated their boilers with coal and many smaller steamers still burn coal in their furnaces to-day. They have crews of sooty-faced men who spend the whole voyage down in the furnace-rooms shoveling coal into the hot blazing furnaces. These men are called stokers. But great liners like ours and all the ships of our navy now burn fuel oil in making their steam. Our tanks hold eight thousand tons of this oil, and our furnaces swallow half a ton every minute. controls the mighty force of the screws. With one twist of our wrist we could stop this great ship, and with another twist we could send it speeding ahead.

There are also deck tennis courts

We spray the oil into the furnaces quickly or slowly as we wish to have more or less steam to turn the machines that move our screws."

The engineer allows us to place our hands on the steel wheel that

The Captain on the bridge tells the engineers just how much steam is wanted. He sends his orders down by means of electric signals. He pushes a lever and straightway the engineers turn the machines as he directs.

There are telephones on our ship so that the Captain can also talk with his officers or his helpers at any time.

Here in this part of the ship we see the whirling dynamos that

Building an Ocean Giant

We are tired with our journey over the ship. We are glad to drop down in our deck chairs and wrap ourselves up in our warm rugs for a short rest before

There is even a swimming pool

make the electricity used to give us our light and heat. Each night away out here on the ocean more than fifteen thousand electric lamps shine forth. Enough current is made to light a city of forty thousand people.

lunch. There is a pleasant-faced man in the chair next to Dick's who is much interested in hearing of our morning's adventures.

"I am a shipbuilder myself, and in my own ship-yard we have built ocean giants almost as big

In the library

as this one," he says. "Perhaps you would like me to tell you how we build ships. A modern ship has many ribs of steel set in a steel backbone that runs along its bottom from one end to the other. Over its steel ribs is fastened its thin skin of steel plates. These are joined so tightly together that they keep

out the water. The plates of this vessel are probably less than an inch and one-half thick. In battleships the steel plates may be ten times thicker, for they must withstand the shots of enemy vessels. When we have the steel framework in place and the plates fastened upon it, the inside of the ship is built in and furnished. This is done much as in a modern hotel."

Our deck-mate tells us that ever since the days of the first steamships, the builders have been trying to make them larger and stronger, and steadier and swifter. Above all, they try to build them for the greatest possible safety. It is for that reason that at the level of the water and below it, the ship's steel shell is double. There is an air space between the steel plates of its sides large enough for a big dog to crawl through. The whole lower part of our vessel is divided into rooms that can be shut away from each other. If a leak should occur in any one room, its water-tight doors could be closed and the ship perhaps saved from sinking.

A Chat with the Captain

The red letter day of our ocean trip is that on which we pay a

The ship has a huge kitchen

visit to the Captain on his bridge over the upper deck. At sea the Captain of a ship is just like a king. He is responsible for the safety of the whole ship and of all the people upon it. His word is law and every one, crew and passengers, too, must obey him.

Great soup pots are boiling

The Captain invites us into the little house on the bridge which he calls the pilot house, so that we may find out how our vessel is steered.

"There are no sign posts on the roads of the sea," the Captain

The ship has a butcher shop, too

says, "we must find our way for ourselves. We guide our ship by the sun, the moon, and the stars just as did the seamen in the days of the Bible. But we dense fogs cover the sky, we can tell where we are going. Then we have an instrument called a sextant with which we can tell just where we are by observing

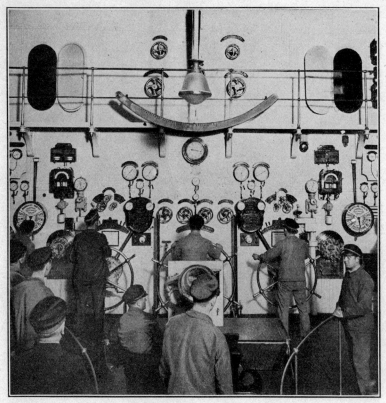

The control board in the engine room

have ways of finding out where we are that they did not have. We have this mariner's compass whose trembling needles are like magnets. They point always towards the north, so even when the sun. And we have a ship's clock that does not go wrong with the pitching and tossing of the boat as an ordinary clock might. This is called a *chronometer*. Perhaps you have noticed that, on a ship, bells sound the time instead of a clock gong. That is because bells can be heard better."

wheel this way and that. He says it is joined with the rudder at the rear of the ship in such a way that as the wheel turns, the

Building a giant ocean liner

One of the ship's officers is on duty as pilot. He stands behind the steering wheel, gazing now out at sea and now down at the glass-covered compass before him. He turns the rudder moves from side to side in the water and so changes the direction in which the ship is going. The pilot is always on the lookout for other ships that may cross his path.

Great Lakes steamers

Kinds of Ships

"Oh, a ship! Look! Over there!" Helen points to a huge steamer far out to our right. smoke stacks instead of three high ones like ours. And there is no trail of smoke drifting behind it. We wonder if its engines

Our ship is one of the largest afloat

The Captain lets us look at it through his strong sea glasses. It seems much like this great vessel upon which we are traveling, except that it has two stubby have stopped. But the Captain tells us that this ship has no smoke. It does not need furnaces to make steam. It is a motor ship. It runs by means of engines with pistons and cylinders somewhat like those in our automobiles. Motor ships have been

A submarine

called the automobiles of the sea because of this fact. Their decks are clean because they have almost no smoke.

We pass a number of ships during our crossing. Some are carrying passengers like us. Others have on board nothing but the crew and a cargo of freight. All the things we buy from far-away lands must come across the ocean to us in ships. And the things we make to sell to our friends over the ocean must be shipped to them in ocean carriers. Freight ships ride lower than passenger vessels. They do not need so much room above the water for decks and for staterooms. Most of a freight ship is given over to space for its bales and its boxes.

Our own ship carries some freight and express. Great rooms down inside its hull are

Submarines can also travel under water

A motor ship — the automobile of the seas

A great gray warship

filled with the automobiles and the cotton, the fruit, and other things we are sending abroad. There is one special part set aside for a post office. There, thousands of sacks of mail are stored and sorted during the voyage.

We all remember our journey on a Great Lakes ore boat. Much freight is carried over these great inland bodies of water. Besides the ore boats, there are freighters for coal and special ships that will each hold almost half a million bushels of grain from our Great Lakes states.

Among the pictures of ships which we place in our Museum are photographs of a great gray battleship and a low submarine. We think it wonderful that these submarines can travel so far down under the water.

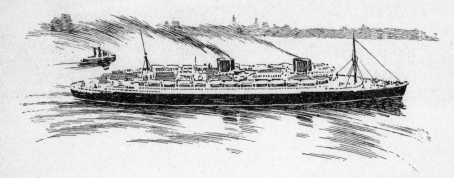

CHAPTER 17

FLYING THROUGH THE AIR

Long, long ago, boys and girls in old Greece believed that there was once a man who flew through the air just like a bird. This man's name was Dædalus. With his son, Icarus, he is said to have flown away from prison on wings made of wax. Dædalus reached safety, but poor Icarus flew too near the hot sun. His wings of wax melted, and he fell into the sea. Another Greek legend about flying through the air is that of the winged horse, Pegasus, who could soar through the clouds and who finally flew away up to Heaven.

Mercury

"The birds can fly, an' why can't I?" asks the farmer's boy in the poem about "Darius Green and His Flying Machine." Mary has brought these verses to read at our Journey Club meeting, for to-day we are to find out just how we can travel in the air high above the earth.

Men have always wanted to fly. For thousands of years they envied the birds skimming across the heavens. They tried and they tried to find out their secret. But it was only a very short while ago — no farther back than our own fathers can remember — that they began to learn about real flying. To-day we can go swiftly from one part of the world to another in huge bird-like planes and giant airships at a speed greater than that of the fastest express train. Most people think that, before we grow up, so much more will have been learned that we shall have even better ways of flying than we have now.

Up in a Balloon

One cold November evening about one hundred and fifty years

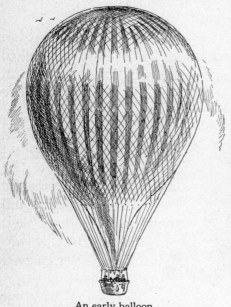

An early balloon

ago two brothers named Montgolfier sat before an open fire in their home in France. As they watched the smoke curl up the chimney, one said to the other: "Why could we not make that smoke carry something along with it into the air?" The Montgolfier family had long been

paper-makers. So it was easy for these brothers to get a specially strong paper bag. They held this bag over a little tin dish on which they had made a smoky fire. To their delight, as soon as their bag was filled with the hot air and the smoke, it rose to the ceiling.

Again and again these Frenchmen worked out tests with paper balloons. They made their bags bigger and stronger. They tried bags of linen as well as of paper. At last they gave a public exhibition. Before a gaping crowd they sent up six thousand feet into the air a huge balloon that weighed as much as two men.

Several months later there was another balloon test. This time the bag was filled with a gas, which, like hot air, is always lighter than cold air. This balloon was escorted by a great parade in which there were hundreds of flaming torches. There was the greatest excitement. A cannon was fired and the balloon rose. Up, up it went until it was lost in the clouds. It came to earth fifteen miles away from Paris where the farmer folk had never heard of a balloon. They thought the strange object must be a monster from another world. Many were afraid and ran away. Some of the braver ones came close enough to shoot it with their guns. As the monster began to shrink, the farmers rushed at it with their pitchforks. At last they tied it to the tail of a horse which galloped away, dragging the balloon. It was soon ripped to bits.

Soon after this still another balloon was sent into the sky. This one carried three live passengers: a sheep, a duck, and a hen. They came safely back to earth and a few months later two men were found who were willing to risk their lives in a balloon trip. They stayed in the air for twenty minutes, floating through the sky over the city of Paris.

Edith's Balloon Ride

Those first balloons were the beginning of men's trips into the air. Bigger and better balloons were made until to-day they can be used to carry passengers and freight for hundreds of miles. One racing balloon sailed through the sky farther than from New

Getting ready for a balloon race

York to Kansas City, Missouri, without coming down. Edith once took a trip in a balloon at a county fair. She tells us about it.

"The bag of my balloon was of cloth," she explains. "It was coated with a rubber varnish and covered with a strong network of cord. I sat in a small wicker basket or car that hung just under the bag. The balloonist told me that our bag was filled with a gas much lighter than the cold air about it. This is what made the balloon rise from the ground. He said that hydrogen gas and a gas called helium are

Now and then, when we wanted to go higher, the balloonist would throw out some of the sand, thus making our balloon lighter. We floated this way and that, going wherever the wind blew us,

The Los Angeles — a dirigible

the ones chiefly used for balloons to-day. Our balloon was tied fast to stakes in the ground. As soon as the ropes were loosed, we rose into the air. There were heavy sand bags hung over the sides of our basket. They weighted the car down so that we should not rise too quickly.

for there was no way to guide the balloon I rode in. When it was time to come down again, we pulled a cord that opened the gas bag at the top. This let out some of the gas that was holding us up in the air and so we drifted gently back to earth."

Balloons like the one in which

Edith rode are not very useful because they cannot be guided. They must drift with the wind. However, a few such balloons were used by officers in the

He throws open the window and cries out in excitement.

"Come! Look! There's an airship flying over us now!" We rush out of the house and stand

Comfortable seats in an air liner

World War in order to get better views of neighboring camps and battlefields.

Ships of the Air

Jack is sitting in a chair next the window. As Edith finishes her story he jumps to his feet.

with our necks craned, peering up into the sky. Sailing across the blue heavens, we see a huge gray fish that shines like silver in the rays of the sun. It is a long cigar-shaped balloon of the kind we call airships. It is held up in the air by means of gas, just as was

We set out for the flying field [Dick, Edith, Helen, and Jack]

Edith's. But in many other ways it is far different. This airship is a dirigible. This means it is a "guidable" balloon. It has powerful gasoline engines to stretched over stiff frames of aluminum and so they are called *rigid* dirigibles. Others have no stiff framework at all. They are known as *non-rigid* dirigibles.

In the kitchen of a dirigible

propel it, and it is so made that it can be steered at the will of its captain.

There are two kinds of guidable, or dirigible, balloons. Some are like the one above us there in the sky. Their coverings are The most noted of these ships of the air are rigid dirigibles called Zeppelins, so named for the German Count Zeppelin who built the first gas bag with a metal framework. Many Zeppelins were used by the Germans in the

World War, and dirigibles, especially the *Graf Zeppelin*, have crossed the wide oceans carrying many passengers and much freight and mail.

Dick has brought a picture of a huge modern airship for our Journey Club Museum. One view shows us that it is built with many little compartments, just like those of the lower part of an ocean steamer. These compartments are each gas-tight. If one should have a leak, the gas would yet stay safely in the others, and the balloon could still float. Another picture of Dick's airship shows us some of the cabins and the other rooms for passengers. There are staterooms with washstands and berths.

AVIATION ROUTING BEACON Nº 320

PILOTS DEPEND ON THIS BEACON FOR THEIR SAFETY

PROPERTY OF U. S. AIR MAIL SERVICE POST OFFICE DEPARTMENT

Lights guide the planes at night

There is a dining room and a sitting room, a kitchen and a pantry. And there is even an inclosed deck with windows of clear glass through which one can look out at the clouds or down at the country side so far below. Dick says his father believes that the time will come when passenger airships will cross the ocean as regularly as steamships do to-day. He thinks they will make the trip in two days.

Airships like the one in these pictures are almost as long as a huge ocean vessel. They cost millions of dollars and they have mighty engines that do the work of thousands of horses all pulling together. It takes a large crew of men to run an airship of this kind.

The Journey Club Flies

Bring a coat or a sweater with you this afternoon! We are going for a trip in a huge airplane and although the day is warm, we may find it chilly so far up there in the clouds.

Our city is on the line of one of the mail and passenger air services of our United States. The

An airport during the day

The same airport at night

plane we are to take will carry us safely off through the air to a big city several hundred miles away west. Little by little all the big cities of our land are being linked that planes may land safely at any hour of the day or night. At one side of the port is a tall beacon light. At night its flashing beams pierce the darkness for

The world below us is one vast map

to each other by such air lines. In Europe to-day there are many passenger air services and every day large numbers of travelers go by air from one great capital to another.

We ride out to the flying field in a motor bus. Our city has just built a fine new airport so miles to show the sky pilots their way to the vast landing field. In another part of the airport is a huge white arrow which whirls round with the wind and so tells the airmen the direction from which the wind is blowing. Those long low sheds over there are the hangars, where planes may be sheltered. On the hangar roofs the name of our city is printed in such large letters that it can be easily read from high in the air.

of the waiting room the great flying machine has rolled up to the door. It stops only long enough to put off and take on its mail, and its passengers.

We examine our plane [Bob, Dick, Mary, Edith, Helen, and Jack]

We buy our tickets in the little waiting room. It reminds us of a railway station in a small town. We sit down on its benches as we wait for our plane. Hark! That whirring noise means that the plane is coming now. Almost before we have time to step out

We climb up through the little door in its side and settle ourselves in low seats by the plane's windows. The pilot, in leather jacket and goggles, slides into his place. The door is closed. The propellers whirl round and with a whirring and roaring the engines start. As we glide off over the ground on our rubber-tired wheels we feel just as though we were riding in an automobile. All at once Jack gives a shout.

like those of a toy village. The people seem to be tiny ants moving about, and the speeding automobiles remind us of crawling beetles. Now we are flying high

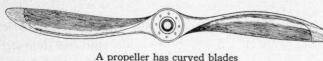

The Langley air plane

"We're off the ground!" he cries. Sure enough! Our wheels have left the earth and we are climbing up into the sky. We

A propeller has curved blades

are surprised to find that this air lane seems quite as solid as the city streets upon which we drive our automobiles. Up, up, up we go! The houses begin to look

over the countryside. The light greens of the fields and the darker greens of the forests look like patchwork quilts, and the roads are mere white lines running between them. Now we are so high that the world below us is spread out like a vast map, showing mountains and valleys, rivers and lakes.

Here comes a cloud! Our windows are covered with mist as we

fly through it. The air grows colder and we pull our coats well up round our necks. On and on we go, now rising, now falling, at the will of our pilot.

See, we are nearing the city where our airplane is to stop next. Its houses grow larger as we come closer. Our plane's nose is headed for a broad patch of green at the city's edge. This is the airport. We read the name of the city on the hangars and seem to dive toward them. With a twist of a lever, our pilot sends our plane coasting gently downward. We hardly know when our wheels first touch the ground. We roll along smoothly over the grass and come to a stop.

A Look at Our Airplane

This is the end of the route for this airplane of ours, so we shall have a chance to chat with our pilot and to examine the wonderful flying machine in which we have traveled. As it stands there on the ground, it looks like a great gray bird with wings outstretched and beak in the air.

Wilbur Wright in his first plane

Our pilot tells us there is a great difference between airships and airplanes. He says the airship, with its huge bags of gas, is lighter than air. The airplane is heavier than the air through which it goes. The one in which we have been riding is a mass of wood, steel, and linen that weighs more than the heaviest automobile. It has no bags of gas to lift it from the ground.

"It is the propeller as well as the wings that makes an airplane fly," the pilot explains. "The first airplanes of all were merely huge kites. They were gliders.

They had no engines. To use them men had to go up on a high hill and glide off into the wind. These early gliders could not be through the air that real flying was possible. You see, a moving airplane stays in the air for the same reason a kite does. As

Airplanes carry our mail

made to stay in the air for more than a few hundred feet. Gliding is not flying as we fly to-day. It is more like easy falling. It was not until men learned to make a gasoline engine turn a propeller and so pull the plane long as its propeller pulls it along at a swift pace, the air presses on the under side of the wings so hard that it keeps it from falling. But the moment its propeller stops whirling around, the plane must come down to earth."

"Who invented the airplane?" Helen asks.

"No one person," is the answer. "German and French inventors who built the very first airplane that carried a man safely up through the air. They discovered the secret of building

Making a map in the air

worked upon it. But the Americans, Samuel P. Langley and Wilbur and Orville Wright, were the ones who really taught the world how to fly. The famous Wright brothers were the most important of all, for it was they airplanes so that they would not tip over in a strong wind. They learned how to curve their wings so that they would be held up by the pushing and pulling of the air currents. It was at their flying ground on the sands of North

Airplanes carry passengers just as trains do

A monoplane

A biplane in flight

Carolina in 1903 that men had their first real lesson in practical flying."

The pilot shows us how the propeller blades are shaped to cut through the air with the motion of a screw. The powerful gasoline engines whirl them about thirty times in one second. Some airplanes have only one motor and one propeller. Others have two or three, like this one of ours. There are several different kinds of airplanes here at this airport. There are machines that have only one broad plane like ours. They are monoplanes. There are also biplanes with two broad linen-covered wings placed one above the other. Triplanes have three wings.

We find that the engines in our

A sea plane

plane are somewhat like that of an automobile except that they are many times more powerful. Our pilot shows us the switchboard just in front of his driving seat in the plane. It reminds us of the dashboard of an automobile. The airman thinks an airplane is as simple to manage as a motor car. He believes that some day we shall each drive our own airplane, just as our fathers now drive their automobiles.

How We Use Airplanes

During the weeks after our trip in the giant airplane, we cut out of the newspapers and the magazines articles showing for how many things we use airplanes. Some tell of passenger planes like that we rode in. Others give the thrilling stories of the mail planes that carry one thousand pounds of air mail from one coast to the other in such a short time. These fly by day and by night. In some places their route is marked by flashing lights in towers built here and there along the way. One cutting tells of the air trucks that are loaded with fast express.

Other articles describe how planes were flown during the World War, and how they are used by our army and navy for protecting our country to-day. Mary brings us an air map. Re-

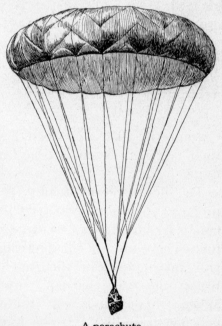

A parachute

membering how clearly we could see the outlines of the fields and the forests, of the cities and towns from our seats in the planes, we can easily understand how useful airplanes might be in making such maps.

Helen has a photograph of the city of Washington that was taken from an airplane. She says the city was photographed in several sections and then the photographs were put together into one whole. This great air photograph was taken in order to help the city planners to

An amphibian

dred pictures were made. These were later fitted together like a giant picture puzzle.

Jack has brought us stories of our sea planes and flying boats. Sea planes are built like airplanes save that they have boat-like

Warships carry airplanes

make Washington more beautiful. There are air cameras that will take photographs from a height of ten thousand feet. When New York was photographed from the air, one hun-

floats in place of rubber-tired wheels. This is so that the plane may land on the water with safety. Flying boats are more like boats with broad wings. They are often called *amphibians*.

Colonel Charles A. Lindbergh and the Spirit of St. Louis

The boy Lindbergh

at sea or in the desert. One of the strangest uses of all is in destroying plagues of insects that ruin the crops of our farmers. Airplanes fly low over their fields, scattering clouds of poison dust or poison gas that kill off the pests.

Our most interesting cutting of all is about a floating airport. This huge vessel can carry more than eighty planes. It has a flat deck longer than the Woolworth

Amelia Earhart

Sea planes and flying boats are useful in patrolling our coasts and in helping fishermen spy out the best fishing grounds. There are special airplanes, too, for travel in the Far North. These have, instead of wheels, giant skis upon which they may safely land upon fields of ice or snow. A plane with skis has been used for flying over the North Pole.

Others of the Journey Club have cuttings that tell of air ambulances, and planes that look for forest fires and for persons lost

Our airplane has three engines [Mary, Helen, Dick, Edith, Bob, and Jack]

Building in New York is tall. From this deck its airplanes can take off or land when their flight has been made. Some day there may be airplane landings here

Commander Richard E. Byrd

and there all the way across the Atlantic Ocean.

Air Heroes

Our Journey Club Museum has a special shelf for our air heroes. Ever since the beginning of flying,

airmen have been trying to fly faster and farther than ever before. Many have given their lives in their effort to help the world to fly better. One of the chief reasons why the airplane is useful is that it goes so much faster than any other means of travel. The ordinary airplane flies through the air at a speed of one hundred miles in an hour, and by using it much valuable time may be saved. The fastest speed through the air was made by an expert airman who flew more than five times as quickly as our fastest express train can travel. Airplanes have reached great heights. One climbed to a distance of more than seven miles up toward the sun.

Beside the pictures of Langley and the Wright brothers, the first airplane makers, we place photographs of some of our most famous flyers. There is Lieutenant Commander A. C. Read of our navy, who was first to fly from America to Europe. There are our army flyers, who flew all the way around the world. Commander (later Rear Admiral)

Richard E. Byrd who was the first to soar in a plane through the air above the North Pole, and later, he was also the first to fly over the South Pole. Perhaps most of all we admire the young hero, Charles A. Lindbergh (later Colonel), who set forth all alone in his plane, the *Spirit of St. Louis*, to go across the stormy Atlantic from New York to Paris without any stop. His feat of daring is still one of the wonders in the story of flying, and our airmen all hope that his is but the first of a great procession of planes that will some day be going regularly back and forth between our land and the lands of our friends over in Europe.

We think that we should like to learn to fly when we are old enough. There are a number of airplane schools where flying is taught. Flying is far safer now than in the early days when planes could go up in good weather only.

CHAPTER 18

A TELEGRAM FOR THE JOURNEY CLUB

The Journey Club is meeting to-day at Helen's home. We are just beginning our program when the door bell rings. Helen excuses herself and goes to see who it is. In a minute she returns, waving a small envelope in the air.

"A telegram for the Journey Club," she cries. She hands the envelope to Mary who tears it open and reads:

Samuel F. B. Morse

```
NEW YORK N Y            19 — MAY 7
THE JOURNEY CLUB
    OUR CITY
        OUR STATE
            SORRY TO BE ABSENT FROM THE
MEETING TODAY   GOOD LUCK
                DICK
```

This message has come to us all the way from New York, where Dick is visiting his aunt. It seems like fairy magic when we think what a short while ago it was that Dick started these words off through the air to us. And lo, here they are, brought to our very door in almost less time than it would take us to trace on our maps the route they have traveled over mountains and valleys, over rivers and plains.

Ever since the days of the caveboy, Strong-as-a-Lion, men have needed to send messages. When

251

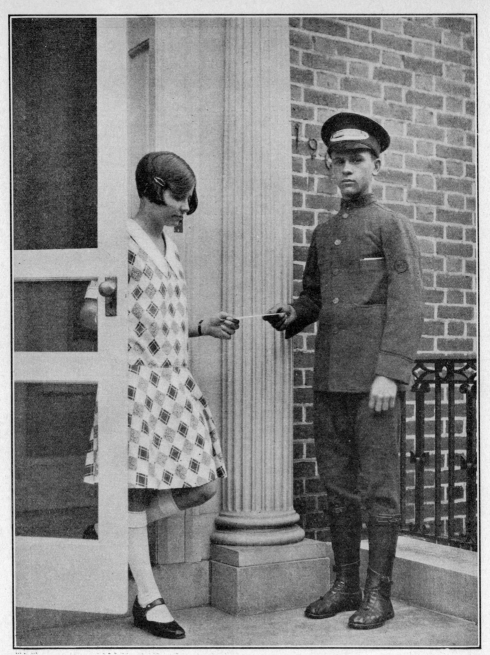

Helen receives a telegram for the Journey Club

Strong-as-a-Lion's father wanted to get word quickly to his brother who lived on a neighboring mountain, he built a smoky fire. By waving an animal hide at the fire he was able to make the smoke blow in certain ways. Standing near his distant cave home, his ways in which messages travel. In some lands drums are beaten so loudly that their signals may be heard in the neighboring villages. In others, warnings of danger or tidings of good fortune are sent from one place to another by tapping on poles set deep in

The Indians sent smoke signals

brother could see and understand these smoke signals, and he sent his answer back in the same fashion. Our own American Indians used to send messages across our plains by means of fires of this kind or lighted torches.

Strange Ways of Sending Messages

At our meeting to-day we are to find out the many different the ground. Certain taps are used to mean certain things. A system of signals for sending messages like these is called a code.

Helen's Uncle Harry has given us some pictures that show us how messages were sent by the soldiers in the World War when there was no telephone or telegraph at hand. In one of these,

Boy Scouts signaling messages

we see a man signaling with flags. He moves the flags to the right or to the left into different positions for each letter of our alphabet. Helen calls this wigwagging. She says either one or two flags may be used. There are special codes for each way of wigwagging. Beside the railroad tracks of our land we often see tall posts with movable arms of metal or wood. Like the wigwagging

flags, these arms are used to carry messages. They tell the engineers on the trains whether or not the tracks are clear. Such signaling posts are called semaphores.

Another of our war pictures shows us a man sending signals with a mirror. A mirror placed in the sun can be made to reflect its bright rays so that they may be seen for long distances. The signals are made up of long and short flashes. They also follow a code. Mirror-signaling is known as *heliographing*. At night a

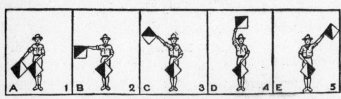

Signaling by flags

The Pony Express

lamp may be used instead of a mirror.

But the photographs we like best of all our war pictures are those of the brave carrier pigeons. These homing birds flew for many miles over the battlefields. They carried thousands of important messages in tiny rolls tied to their slender legs.

Bob tells us the story of the runners of olden times who sped so swiftly over the roads of Greece and Rome, and Mary reminds us of the Pony Express whose daring riders galloped with the mail from one western

The Greeks sent messages by runners

American settlement to another in the days before the railroads came. In our journeys to find out about ourselves and our city we have already seen how the United States Post Office carries messages for us in the form of letters and postal cards.

long distances over electric wires. Many men were working on this problem, but as yet none had found out the secret. Mr. Morse had a plan that he thought might succeed where theirs had failed. So he gave up his painting and devoted his days to studying the

Sending one of the first telegrams

The First Telegraph Message

One day, about a hundred years ago, an American artist, named Samuel F. B. Morse, landed in New York from a trip to Europe. He was filled with excitement, for during his journey there had occurred to him the wonderful idea that messages might some day be sent for

wonders of electricity. For three years he made tests with electric currents and little magnets treated with electricity. At last he learned to join the wires and magnets together in such a way that clicking sounds could be heard at each end of long wires. In 1835 he showed to the world the first telegraph instrument.

But even after this mighty secret had been discovered, Mr. Morse's hardest work still lay before him. Every one laughed at his invention. They would Congress voted him thirty thousand dollars. With this money he set up the poles and strung the wires for a forty-mile telegraph line between Washington

A modern telegraph office

not believe it could be useful. No one would lend him the money he needed to build telegraph lines. It took him eight years to interest the United States Government in his great idea. Finally, in 1843; and Baltimore. On May 24, 1844, he sent over this line the words, "What hath God wrought." This was the very first telegraph message.

Gradually telegraph lines were

put up in all parts of the United States and in other countries as well. We Americans telegraph more than any other nation. One-third of all the telegraph poles on the globe are on American soil. We send more messages

Telegrams are sent over wires

by wire than the larger European nations put together. Every twelve months hundreds of millions of messages are flashed over our wires.

No matter what state we may go through on our Journey Club trips, we shall see everywhere tall telegraph poles of chestnut or cedar or strong yellow pine.

Each of these poles has a number of wooden crossarms fastened to it. And standing like soldiers on the crossarms are rows of glass-capped wooden pins that hold the wires. The little glass caps around which the wires pass keep the flashing electric messages from running off down the wooden poles into the ground, for electricity cannot make its way through glass.

The Story of Our Telegram

We decide that a part of our club program to-day shall be to send an answer to Dick's telegram. The easiest way would be to use Helen's telephone to call the telegraph office. We could then pay her father the amount that would be charged for it on his telephone bill. But we think we would rather go down town ourselves so that we may see just how a telegram is sent.

Jack writes our message on a telegraph blank at one of the little desks in the telegraph office.

We hand it to the young man behind the high wooden counter and we pay him a few cents for

Our message is started

each word we are to send. We are told that telegrams are often sent collect, the ones who receive them paying the bill.

We ask if we may not watch our telegram start off over the wires. The young man introduces us to a girl who is sitting before a little machine that reminds us of a typewriter. She looks at our message, and with flying fingers she taps it off on the keys of this machine. She shows us how with each tap the machine punches a group of holes in a strip of tape. Every letter of our alphabet has a certain group of these holes that stand for it in the telegraph alphabet.

Look at the tape passing through that other little machine that joins the one which our operator is using! This is the *transmitter*, or *sender*. The operator explains that the transmitter sends out over the wires certain electric signals for each group of punched holes. In the office in New York another wonderful machine will change these electric signals back into letters again. At the same time it will print our message on a telegraph

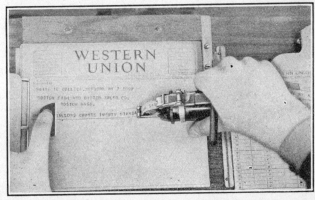

A message is printed on a strip of paper

blank, or on a strip of gummed paper which a girl will stick on a blank. Then the telephone or a speeding messenger boy will deliver our message to Dick.

New York has many telegraph stations. To help their telegrams reach the end of their journeys more quickly, New York and other big cities have laid down underground tubes. Through these tubes telegrams can be shot by compressed air from one part of a city to another in the wink of an eye.

In the small country station near Edith's farm, the telegraph operator sits before a table on which there is a little telegraph instrument. This has a flat round

In some large cities messages can be sent through underground tubes

key which he moves up and down to send his telegrams. The key is used to make the long and short clicks of the telegraph code, as it sends off electric signals over the wires. When a message comes in, a sounder clicks away all by itself while the operator listens carefully and writes down its message.

The girl we are watching tells us that in the past all telegrams were sent in that way. To-day most are tapped out on machines like hers. She says that in some of the largest cities there is still another kind of telegraphing machine which does not punch holes in a tape. It writes its messages out just like a typewriter. It is so made that with each tap of its keys the right electric signal goes forth over the wires. It is like a powerful typewriter with keys hundreds and thousands of miles long. When the operator taps a letter upon it, in less than a second that letter is printed on a strip of gummed

Some sending machines look like typewriters

paper or a telegraph blank at the distant place to which the message is being sent.

At the same time and over the same wire upon which our telegram will travel, three other messages will speed along as if on different paths. One of these wonderful telegraph wires can carry four messages in each direction at the same moment without getting them mixed up.

The Telegraph Alphabet

We are interested in the telegraph alphabet. When Mr. Morse found he could send sharp little clicks over electric wires, he discovered the secret of the tele-graph. But he had also to work out a telegraph code so as to make these clicks mean something. The Morse alphabet is far different from the alphabet we use in spelling. It is made up entirely

"How long does it take a message to reach New York?" Bob asks.

"That depends on how hurried you are," is the operator's answer. "If you wish it sent in the quickest way, it should go as a *Telegram*. Then it will be in New

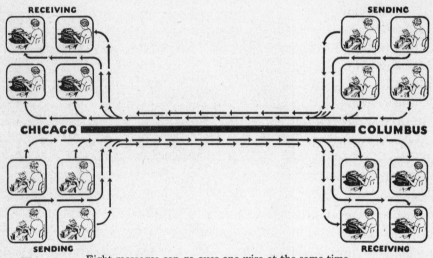

Eight messages can go over one wire at the same time

of short clicks and long clicks which stand for dots and dashes. Each group of these is the symbol for a letter of our alphabet. By putting them together in just the right way, they will spell any word in our dictionary. Our operator shows us how our club name would look in the Morse Code.

J O U R N E Y

C L U B

York in a very few minutes. If you are not so rushed, you might send a *Day Letter*. This takes somewhat longer, but you could use more words, for the rate is cheaper. If you wish to send a very long message, and delivery on the following morning will do, send it as a *Night Letter*. At night our wires are less busy and a night letter of fifty words may be sent for the price of a ten-word telegram during the day. A *Night Letter* is always delivered early the next morning."

The Wonders of the Telegraph

During our visit to the telegraph office we find out in how many wonderful ways the telegraph serves us. In the early days, people sent telegrams only when something dreadful had happened. When the messenger boy brought a telegram to the door, our grandmothers grew pale with fright, for they were sure some one was ill. To-day telegrams are used on all occasions. We may send greetings to our friends on special days such as Christmas, Easter, or Valentine's day. We may telegraph birthday wishes, and when we go on long trips we may send telegrams home to tell of our safe arrival.

Beside our own personal messages, these humming wires are used to flash the news of the world to our daily papers, and to bring our farmers and sailors the weather reports from Washington that tell them when rains or storms are ahead. All railroad stations have their own telegraph operators who click out messages to the other stations along the routes the trains travel. Sometimes they may wish to stop a train because of an accident on down the track. Warning words can fly over these wires faster than the fastest express.

Hundreds of millions of dollars are sent each year from place to place by means of telegraphic

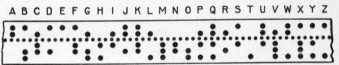

The Morse Code for the alphabet

money orders, and in business offices all over our land the telegraph is used daily. To many busy men the saving of a few minutes in getting a message may mean the saving of thousands of dollars.

Cables under the Sea

More wonderful to us even than these telegraph wires that take our messages into all parts of our land are the telegraph cables that run under the sea. Jack has brought us a picture of the ship that laid the first real cable across the Atlantic Ocean and also a picture of Cyrus Field, the man who succeeded in doing this great work.

One day Cyrus Field was sitting before a globe looking at Ireland and Newfoundland. They seemed to lie so close to each other that he thought there should be a telegraph line from back and forth under the ocean between our own President and the Queen of England. This cable was the first of the many that now encircle the globe. We can send a cable message to almost any nation on earth and our words will speed around the world in a very few minutes. A

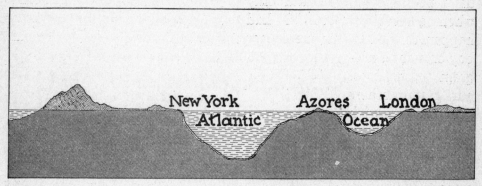

Cables lie along the bottom of the sea

one to the other. His friend, Samuel Morse, had already sent messages on wires under the Hudson River, and an underwater telegraph line was being used between England and France across the English Channel.

Cyrus Field worked twelve years before he finished the task he had undertaken. His cables broke again and again. But he did not give up. At last in 1858 messages were successfully flashed message was once sent from New York to Australia in just three ticks of a watch. A cable message can be flashed to Great Britain and an answer received in less than four minutes.

The cable alphabet is made up of dots and dashes, too, but it is not exactly like the Morse Code. When a cable message is received on the other side of the ocean, it looks like a wavy line. The cable operator knows how to read this as easily as you read this book. Cable messages cost more than telegrams. So special codes have been made up in which one word often stands for a whole sentence. In this way long messages may be made up of valleys and hills. Sometimes these are rocky. In such places the cable is wrapped with strong steel wires to keep the sharp rocks from wearing it through.

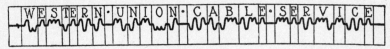

The cable alphabet

sent at a low cost. Cable Letters and Week End Letters which go more slowly are even cheaper.

The cable lines that rest on the bed of the ocean must be well protected. The copper wires through which the electric signals are flashed lie in the heart of a great

Jack tells us that each ocean cable was laid by a great ship that sailed slowly over its route. Machinery on board unwound the cable which was stored in a vast tank inside the ship. The cable dropped down under the sea as the ship steamed along. He says

How a cable wire is protected

cable. Several waterproof overcoats of rubber are wrapped tight around these wires. Then another coating of a fiber called *jute* is put on. Next comes a layer of heavy steel wires and last of all a wrapping of yarn and other materials. The bed of the ocean is when the cable is laid a careful record is kept of its location and depth. In case it breaks at any point along the route, a repair ship can steam straight to the spot, pick up the broken ends with grappling hooks and join them again.

CHAPTER 19

THE STORY OF THE TELEPHONE

Our visit to the telegraph office is over. We are again walking along the crowded sidewalks in the busiest section of our city. We are on our way to the home of another of our trusted messengers, the telephone. Before we left Helen's house we called up Mr. Earle, a cousin of Mary's who works in the office of our telephone company. He is in charge of the Information Department and he has promised to help us find out all about the wonderful way in which our voices are carried for such long distances over the telephone wires.

"Your telephone is one of the best servants you have," says Mr. Earle when we have seated ourselves in chairs round his desk. "It carries more than seventy times as many messages as its sister, the telegraph. When you are sick you call the doctor by 'phone. If your house catches fire or burglars break in, the quickest way to get help is by telephoning for the firemen or the police. Your mother orders much of her food and other household supplies over the telephone. Your school and your church must have telephones to help them to run smoothly. The news in your newspapers is much of it sent in over the telephone wires. Every factory and store, every bank, mill, and mine depends chiefly on the telephone to

1876
Bell Telephone

An early telephone

266

The telephone is our friend and servant

Business men must have telephones

any city of the United States, with persons in Canada and Mexico, and even with friends across the ocean in the great cities of Europe. Some day we shall perhaps be able to send our voices all the way around the world."

The Birth of the Telephone

"Mr. Watson, please come here; I want you." These were the first words that were ever spoken through a telephone. Mr. Earle tells us the story of how the telephone

carry its messages. So, you see, everything you eat, wear, and use every day has been helped on its way to you by the telephone."

"What did people do when they did not have telephones?" Jack asks.

"Your grandfathers or your grandmothers could answer that question," is Mr. Earle's reply. "They can remember when the telephone was unheard of. In those days, when they wanted to talk with a friend, they had to put on their hats and coats and go forth to find him. To-day you and I can sit comfortably in our own homes or at our own desks and chat with almost any one in

Alexander Graham Bell

was born in 1875 in the little workshop of the young Boston schoolteacher, Alexander Graham Bell. He describes the many months of experiments which Mr. Bell and his assistant, Mr. Watson, had made, in their efforts to improve on the new telegraph. Mr. Bell was trying to make a telegraph instrument that would send several messages at one time over the same wires. But he was even more interested in finding out how to carry the sound of the human voice from one place to another by wire.

At last one day over his wires there came a tiny sound made by his assistant in another room. At that moment he knew he had found out the secret of the telephone.

Alexander Graham Bell had about as much trouble as Samuel Morse in getting people to believe in his new invention. They called him a "crank who says he can talk through a wire." They often hooted at him during his first lectures when he tried to show off his wonderful instrument. Even when he proved

that it would work, they thought this "box that talked" merely an electrical toy. The very first telephone was a receiver and sender all in one, and the first

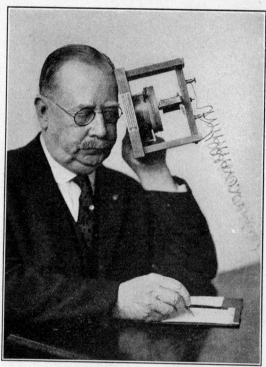

A model of Bell's first telephone

telephone conversations were sent over borrowed telegraph lines. It was not until much later that Mr. Bell raised enough money to form a telephone company that put up its own telephone poles and wires. We laugh when Mr. Earle tells us that in those early days one called to the telephone operator as to a ship, by shouting, "Ahoy," instead of saying, "Hello."

Telephone Fairies

In order to show us better how our telephone works, Mr. Earle asks if one of our club will not make a call. Mary takes the desk 'phone in her hands. She lifts the receiver from its hook and waits for a second. Then we hear her say, "North 6573."

In another moment she speaks again into the mouthpiece.

"Hello," she says; "this is Mary, Mother. We are at the office of the Telephone Company. May I please bring the girls and boys home for supper? . . . . That's fine! Good-bye."

"Now I will tell you just what happened when Mary was

Helen speaks over the telephone

telephoning," Mr. Earle says. "Let me pretend that I am this telephone instrument here before us. I will tell you its story as though it were really speaking. We telephones are fairies. We work magic more wonderful than that of Titania. This mouthpiece is my ear. With it I take in the words you speak to me. I lay my spell on your words and I change them into electric waves which speed swiftly and silently over my copper wires. Quick as a flash these electric waves flow into the receiver of the telephone instrument at the other end of those wires. That instrument is another fairy like me. It breaks the spell I have cast and changes the waves I have sent back again into the words you have spoken. Its receiver is its mouth. From it come the sounds of the words just as clearly and as loud as was your voice when you gave them into my ear."

What Happened when Mary Telephoned

"When Mary lifted my receiver from its hook," Mr. Earle goes on, "a tiny light flashed on the switchboard of the telephone

A telephone switchboard

office that serves this part of our city. The quick eye of the girl operator sitting in front of that panel in the switchboard caught the gleam of the light. Her nimble fingers picked up a little plug fastened on the end of a long cord. She thrust this into a tiny hole just beside the light. That hole belongs to me. My two

In a telephone exchange

copper wires run straight from this desk down into the telephone office and into that hole. There are thousands of holes like mine on the switchboards of our city. Every telephone has its own special 'jack,' as these holes are called. And each jack has the number of its 'phone printed beside it.

"In the cord which the operator plugged into my jack were wires that ran to her own telephone receiver. When our wires were thus joined, her words, 'Number, please!' flowed through my receiver into Mary's ear. You all saw how short a time it took the operator to plug into my jack the wires that lead to Mary's own telephone. With a push of a tiny lever, the operator made

Mary's bell ring. This brought her mother to the 'phone so that Mary could talk with her. If the line had been busy, a tiny buzzing noise would have warned the operator not to interrupt."

Mr. Earle says that one big exchange is usually large enough to take care of all the telephones in a town. But in a city like ours, several are needed. He says the telephone company divides our city into sections with separate telephone exchanges. Each exchange is like the exchange of a small town. These telephone towns have their own names. Mr. Earle's 'phone belongs in the telephone town called Main while Mary's 'phone is in North. The operators all help each other in bringing together the wires and the 'phones of the different telephone towns.

Some factories are so large that they may each need hundreds of telephones. They have their own switchboards and their own operators.

In some places, too, the tele-

phones are built so that operators are not needed. Each instrument has a little disc with numbers from zero to nine printed upon it. By whirling this disc around with the finger any number may be

A telephone and its parts

called and the right wires joined together. Such telephone systems are called automatic because they work by themselves.

Where Our Telephones Came From

"You could never guess how many different things are needed to make us telephones work." Mr. Earle is again speaking as though he were the telephone.

"Poles from the forests," says Edith.

"Wires from the copper mines," cries Bob.

"Glass caps for the wooden pins that hold the wires on the poles," says Jack, remembering what we have found out about telegraph wires.

"But those are not half," says Mr. Earle. "To make your telephones, you must have cotton to wrap the wires that carry our electric waves, silk for the cords that join our instruments to the boxes on the walls, and wool for the pads under desk telephones. Then there must be gold, silver, and platinum, aluminum and zinc, tin, nickel, and iron, and mica and asphalt. Lead and antimony are two other metals that are used in our parts. Our receivers, our mouthpieces and

A street with wires above ground

parts of our switchboards are made of baked rubber, and each of our wires that runs under the ground is wrapped in thin paper. Beside all these things you must not forget the wood and the stone, the iron and the steel that are needed for telephone buildings. Perhaps most important of all are the thousands of men and women who work day and night to keep your telephones in order so that you may talk at any hour you wish."

Edith asks Mr. Earle how the wires from all the houses of our city get into the telephone offices.

"Out in the country where I live," she says, "the wires are run on poles. But here in the city not a pole is to be seen."

In reply Mr. Earle hands around two pictures of the same street in New York. One shows it when the telephone wires were all carried overhead. In the other he says the wires go through tubes under the ground. We can easily see that underground wires are the best. They do not get in the way, and they do not spoil the looks of our streets. Mr. Earle explains that each wire is carefully wrapped in special paper that keeps its messages from getting mixed up with those of its neighbors. It is then twisted about its twin that belongs to the same 'phone. Several hundreds of these twin wires may be put into one overcoat, or cable, of lead. This protects them and keeps them from breaking.

Long Distance

We walk about the telephone building with Mr. Earle. He shows us the switchboard where

The same street with wires under ground

Mary's call was put through. We stand behind the row of operators, listening to the clicks of their plugs in the jacks and the the murmur of their voices as they say, "Number, please," or "Thank you." Our heads fairly swim as we look at the switchboards with their thousands of tiny holes and their flashing lights. Each operator has her receiver clamped on her head and her telephone mouthpiece hung in front of her lips. This leaves her hands free. How her fingers fly as she plugs first this, then that plug into the jacks! There seems to be a maze of cords on this switchboard, joining people in different parts of our city together so that they may talk with each other.

Especially interesting to us are the girls who are putting through the long distance calls. Here is one who has just joined a telephone in our city with one in Denver, Colorado. Another is

There are many wires in a cable

seen how far our telephones can carry the sound of our voices. Over its wonderful wires we can talk to friends thousands of miles away as easily as to our next door neighbors.

"In 1915," Mr. Earle says, "Alexander Graham Bell in New York held the first coast to coast telephone conversation. Then, as on that eventful day forty years before, he said, "Mr. Watson, please come here, I want you." Mr. Watson, three thousand miles away in San Francisco, laughed and replied over the

now calling a number in New York. And still another is timing a conversation with Miami, Florida. Mr. Earle whispers to us that the name *telephone* comes from two words, "tele" and "phone." These mean "far" and "sound." We think the name good, for we have just

wires, "It will take me almost a week to get there this time." A still more important long distance conversation was held in 1927, when, by the aid of the telephone and the radio, an American in New York talked across the Atlantic with an Englishman in London.

Telephone Miracles

During our visit at the telephone office we hear of wonders so great that we think them miracles. Mr. Earle shows us a photograph that was sent for three thousand miles over telephone lines. He says pictures like this may be carried by telegraph as well as by telephone. Even more wonderful is the invention by which one may see the person to whom he is telephoning. Seeing at a distance is called television, or "far-seeing." In 1927 the president of the American Telephone and Telegraph Company in New York talked by 'phone to Herbert Hoover in Washington, more than 200 miles away. The president of the telephone company was able to see clearly the face of Mr. Hoover as he talked. This proved to the world that electricity could be used to carry sight as well as sound.

These telephone miracles are the work of our American inventors. Most of the improvements that have been thought out for Mr. Bell's first American telephone have been made in our land. We are the greatest telephone users of the whole world, for almost three-fourths of all the telephones belong to us. In 1927 three new 'phones were put in every two

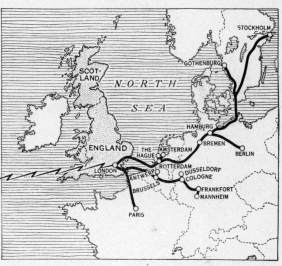

Messages over the ocean travel by telephone and wireless

minutes, and one mile of new wire was run every six seconds day in and day out all the year through. We have enough telephone wire on American soil to reach to the moon nearly 240 times. At first most of our telephones were used for business only. But to-day more then two-thirds are in our homes. Edith has found out that nearly half of the farms of

Herbert Hoover, thirty-first president, talks and sees over the telephone

the United States have telephones. She says the telephone

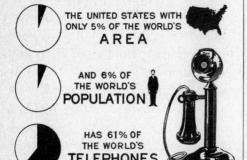

THE U.S. HAS 10 TIMES ITS SHARE
OF THE WORLD'S TELEPHONES

THE UNITED STATES WITH
ONLY 5% OF THE WORLD'S
AREA

AND 6% OF
THE WORLD'S
POPULATION

HAS 61% OF
THE WORLD'S
TELEPHONES

means perhaps more on a far away farm than anywhere else. It puts the lonely farmer in touch with his friends on other farms and with the rest of the world. The telephone is often called "the nation's great neighbor-maker."

Indeed, nothing makes us feel further away or more lost than to be out of reach of a telephone. We like to have one at hand in case of sickness or any other need.

CHAPTER 20

A RADIO TALK

Mary's father is turning over the pages of his evening newspaper. We have just finished a merry supper with Mary's family and we are now gathered in her living room talking over again the things we have found out about some of the wonderful ways in which our messages travel today.

"Well, well," exclaims Mary's father suddenly. "Here is a notice that I am sure is meant for the Journey Club. In a very few minutes there is to be a radio program that will tell of a still more wonderful way in which we can send messages speeding off through the air. It says: '7 : 00 P.M. Station XYZ, A Talk about Radio.' It is now almost seven. Turn on our radio, Mary, and let us hear about it."

Mary pushes a button in the side of the fine big radio set. She twists the little dials to their proper positions. Hardly has she taken her seat in our circle again, before out of the

A microphone

Mary's radio and loud speaker

loud speaker comes a voice as clear and distinct as that of any one of us who might speak in this room. Listen to what it says:

Ladies and Gentlemen of the Radio Audience:

I am going to talk to you for a half hour to-night about one of the greatest wonders of the world. I am going to tell you how it is that I can stand here in our New York studio, hundreds of miles from many of my listeners, and by speaking in an ordinary tone, can send forth my message to all parts of our great land.

No doubt every one who is listening in on my talk to-night knows all about the telegraph and the telephone with their wonderful wires over which messages flash. My story is about another kind of telegraph and telephone. It is about telegraphing and telephoning without any wires. It tells about Radio.

It was a German named Heinrich Hertz who first found out how to send electric waves through the air without wires. He learned that the ether, as the space around the earth is called, is in some ways just like a vast pool of water. When we throw a stone into a pool, little waves ripple out from it in circles that grow wider and wider. An electric splash in the ether acts in just the same way. It sends thousands of electric waves speeding out from it in every direction.

Marconi's Wireless

A young Italian electrician named Guglielmo Marconi became interested in these electric waves. His study finally showed him how to make them work for us in sending messages. With his delicate instruments he learned to flash out into the air the dots and the dashes of the telegraph alphabet, and to pick them up

A radio announcer

again in another part of the world. He was the inventor of the wireless telegraph.

First Marconi flashed his signals to a point one mile away; then for five miles and farther; and now they go half the distance around the world. It was in 1901 that he succeeded in sending his first signal over the ocean. This first signal was just the three short dots that stand for the letter S. Three years later he flashed a complete message through the

The Eiffel Tower is a wireless station

air from one side of the Atlantic to the other.

At first no one paid much attention to the young Italian inventor's wireless signals. However, he did succeed in getting his instruments placed on a few ocean-going vessels. Then about six years later, two huge steamships, the *Republic* and the *Florida,* ran into each other far out at sea. Through the blackness of midnight there flashed forth from the *Republic* the first wireless call for help in a shipwreck. It was heard and answered in time to save fifteen hundred people from going down with the sinking ship. The world was thrilled at this feat. Every steamship line began to plan for wireless outfits for their vessels, and to-day about ten thousand ships have radios on board. Our Government has made a law that all ships carrying fifty persons or more must have a wireless outfit.

Then in 1914 came the terrible World War. Cables can be cut or torn loose by enemy vessels. But no one can stop signals sent through the air. So the nations turned to the use of the wireless telegraph for sending their important messages across the wide seas. In 1915 wireless signals were flashed from the United States across the Atlantic Ocean to France and over the Pacific to far off Hawaii. These were the first of the hundreds and thousands of radiograms that go back and forth over the oceans every day now. Some people use the wireless telegraph instead of the cable lines when they wish to reach friends abroad. Many radiograms are sent by travelers on ships crossing the oceans.

without any wires. But most of us did not realize what could be done in this way until 1920. In that year the earliest radio station, KDKA in Pittsburgh, Pennsylvania, broadcast its first musical program. This event

A wireless station near the ocean

The Wireless Telephone

My voice is coming to you this evening not by the wireless telegraph with its dots and its dashes, but by wireless telephone. We had known for a long time that the sounds of a voice or of music could be sent through the air

was a great success. With it there came into the minds of radio men pictures of thousands of families sitting about in their living rooms listening to concerts, to lectures and plays, to sermons and speeches just as you are listening to me. One by one, more

Grandmother enjoys the radio

and more broadcasting stations were set up, and more and more programs were sent out over the air.

Owners of the early radio sets were often most interested in reaching far distant stations. They bent for hours over their sets, turning the dials this way and that. Now and then, amid shrill squawking, would come the faint words, "Chicago," "New York," or "San Francisco." The listeners would marvel at the miracle of hearing a voice that had traveled so far. But now we have all grown used to these wonderful radio waves that bring sounds to us over the mountains and lakes, through the fields and the forests, and even through the thick walls of our houses. We have so often heard voices from a thousand miles off that we are more interested in the messages they bring.

Our Radio Programs

At first the radio programs were usually given by means of a phonograph played into the microphone. In those days it was easy to set up a broadcasting tower and the number of stations grew very fast. So many programs were on the air that they were often mixed up. The Government at Washington found it must limit the number of stations. It now gives each radio station its own permit or license. Each one is allowed certain letters by which it may be known and called. Every radio operator, too, must have his license. Soon it was found that many stations could comfortably use the same program at the same time. By banding together they could pay enough to have better artists and speakers sing and talk for their programs.

I wish every person who is listening to me could be here in our studio to see just how a radio program is broadcast. I am sitting in front of a metal disc called a microphone. Like a telephone, the microphone takes the sounds I send into it and turns them into electric waves. These waves go out into the air from the network of wires strung on the tower high over our Radio Building. On, on, on through the air they go, crossing the wires that lead into your radio set. Perhaps these are aërials strung above the roof of your home. Or perhaps they are wires wound round a frame just over your set. The wires catch a tiny part of the traveling waves. They carry them straightway into your radio. If your dials are set right, the waves are caught and changed back again into the words I am speaking. All this is done as quick as a flash of lightning, for these electric waves travel so fast that they would go almost seven times round the world in one second's time.

The waves from our station have a certain length. Those from other stations must have different lengths so that our programs shall not be mixed up. You can tune in on almost any station you wish by setting the dials for the right wave length. The wave lengths and programs are given in the daily newspapers.

In a Broadcasting Studio

The room I am in is a broadcasting studio. It is closed tight as a drum. Its floor is padded with cork and its doors are sound proof. I get fresh air from a

Opera singers broadcast their voices

special ventilating machine. There is a glass window in one side of the studio. Through it I see the radio operator who is directing the machine that sends my words through the air to you. He watches me through the glass. Through his machine he listens to each word I speak to be sure it is going out strong and clear over the air.

There are several other studios here in our Radio Building. Each has its piano. In the largest of all is a stage with room enough upon it for a whole orchestra or a grand opera company. There are dressing rooms, shower baths, and reception rooms for the radio artists. Besides these there are, also, the many offices where the business of this great broadcasting company is done.

Not all the programs that come to you from the air are sent out from studios. Some are from the stages of theaters or opera houses where microphones have been set up. Others come from concert halls and public gatherings, from banquets and meetings. Still others are sent out from private homes or from offices. The President of the United States can sit comfortably at his desk in the White House and talk to millions of our people at the same time. It is in this way that he broadcasts his Thanksgiving messages and his Fourth of July greetings to us.

At our studio the same program is often sent out in two ways at one time. It is flashed off the wireless towers for those whose radio sets are near enough to get the program direct. It is also sent over the long distance telephone into the microphone of a station in another city which broadcasts it again for its own listeners. Two stations joined like this by long distance telephone are said to be "hooked-up."

Sometimes, for an especially fine program, as many as sixty stations will join in one great "hook-up." Again, by using the long distance telephone wires, artists in different parts of our land may take part in the same program. On one occasion a speaker sitting in his California home introduced singers in Chicago, New Orleans, and New York to a radio audience of thirty million people in many parts of the world.

An orchestra broadcasting a program from our studio

Weather forecasts are broadcast

How the Radio Serves Us

I wonder if you know all the ways in which the radio serves the men, women, and children of our United States. A glance at the radio page of your newspaper will tell you of its concerts, its lectures and plays, of its health exercises, and its bed-time stories for children. There are often radio accounts of baseball and football games, or of boxing matches. At certain hours the exact time is given so that your clocks may be kept right to the minute.

Radio warns the sailors and farmers of coming storms or freezing weather. It gives the prices that farm produce is bringing in the big markets. Our Department of Agriculture at Washington holds farm school courses over the radio. It broadcasts lessons about crops, about chickens and cattle, about pigs, and other subjects that interest the farmers. These lessons may be studied by the farmers during their long winter evenings. Radio has done much for the farmer's wife,

Radio in the Far North

A radio concert in an airship

too. Those who live in lonely places and those who lie sick in our hospitals may now have all the news of the world as well as music and laughter brought to them through the air.

During a war the radio is used for sending all kinds of messages. From place to place on land, and from the earth to the sky, where brave airmen battle, its messages go. Lost persons are often found by the aid of a radio appeal and many lives have been saved by a radio call for a doctor or medicine. If you should fall ill at sea, and wish to send word to your own doctor on land you may do

so by radio. Then he can tell

A photograph sent by radio

you by wireless just how to cure your disease.

You have no doubt heard of photographs sent by telegraph or telephone. Such pictures may now be sent also by wireless. Carried on the waves of the radio,

a friend in London? If you have, did you know that your voice was carried the greater part of the way by radio? Your telephone wires took it to the broadcasting station on our Atlantic coast. There your voice

Watching a radio movie

a photograph, drawing, or map can cross the Atlantic in a few minutes time. The wonderful machine for television allows you to see the person to whom you telephone. This new invention for seeing at a distance depends on the radio, for these living pictures travel by means of radio waves.

Have you ever telephoned to

was made two billion times louder than when you speak naturally, and radio waves sent it from the tall wireless towers three thousand miles over the water to the receiving station in England. There again telephone wires picked it up and brought it to the friend whom you were calling.

There is no country on the globe where the radio serves the

people so well as here in America. We have almost twice as many radio stations as the other lands of the world all put together. Americans do not have to pay a penny for their wonderful programs, while in England and the rest of Europe each radio set is taxed to help meet the cost of the air entertainments. It is our big business houses and our factories and mills that supply many of the programs that come to you through the air. They do this to help advertise their wares.

As you sit in your cheery homes, listening to your radio, do not forget that there are thousands of men and women working to give you these programs you enjoy. Besides the artists who sing and speak for you, there are the announcers, the operators and their assistants, the line men, and the switch

men. Sometimes two thousand men are needed to help put across one program over a great chain of radio stations.

A modern radio station

Now, Ladies and Gentlemen, my talk is over. I bid you good evening. Please stand by for your own station announcer, who will introduce to you the next feature.

APPENDIX

SUGGESTIONS TO TEACHERS

The following suggestions to teachers are divided for convenience into two groups: first, the general suggestions applicable to all parts of the book ; and second, the special suggestions which apply to particular chapters.

GENERAL SUGGESTIONS

The Journey Club. — It is important that a real club be formed with officers elected by the children. These officers may be changed every few chapters. Records should be kept of the trips made. Projects relating to subjects other than transportation and communication — such as reading, silent or aloud, composition, arithmetic, etc. — may be introduced by the teacher.

The Journey Club Museum. — The value of the Museum cannot be overestimated. A set of shelves provides the place for the exhibits. The actual work of collecting the material and arranging the exhibits should be done by the children, but suggestions as to material available for this purpose will be found both in the text and in the special suggestions that follow.

Maps and Pictures. — There should be two large maps in the schoolroom, one showing the whole world and one showing the United States. Upon the world map should be traced the routes traveled by the children and by the things imported for their daily use. Upon the map of the United States there should be outlined the principal railroad systems, the chief waterways, and the main air routes. Small flags and colored pins will be found effective in locating centers of industry and the birthplaces of the outstanding figures in the history of transportation and communication.

An interesting project may be developed, as the study of these subjects progresses, in the making of a large map of the world, upon which the various means of transportation and communication are shown pictorially. Small drawings or pictures cut from the magazines may be used to indicate characteristic means of travel in specific localities ; such as a dog sled and a reindeer sled in Alaska, a jinrikisha in Japan, a sedan chair in India, steamships of various kinds on the oceans, railroad trains near Chicago, an automobile at Detroit, telegraph poles here and there, etc. This map project may be modeled upon the ancient maps in which such pictorial devices were used to characterize certain places.

Photographs and illustrative material should be obtained wherever possible. The children will find pertinent illustrations in the magazines and the daily newspapers, while the teacher will often receive valuable coöperation from manufacturers and commercial companies whose business is based on transportation and communication needs.

Blackboard and Clay and Sand Tables. — The blackboard may be used for drawings. Clay will be found useful in reproducing the vehicles in which man travels. The sand table will serve to show whole scenes, such as travel in the Far North, travel in Colonial days, a country telephone line, laying a railroad, an automobile show, an airport, etc.

Excursions. — Wherever possible, the children should make the trips suggested in the text, duplicating the experiences there described.

SPECIAL SUGGESTIONS FOR PROJECT PROBLEMS

Chapter 1. — The Journey Club should meet to elect officers for the year. New shelves should be provided in the Museum for the Transportation and Communication Exhibits. A list of new members should be made.

For the Museum: Pictures and models of animals arranged in the order of their respective speed in travel; models of Strong-as-a-Lion's drag; of a drag-cart with a roller beneath its two poles; of a cave man sitting astride a floating log.

Chapter 2. — The pictorial map described in the *General Suggestions* should be begun, each means of travel mentioned in this chapter being depicted thereon. This chapter may be dramatized, every country visited being represented by a child in costume who tells the story of transportation in that land.

For the Museum: A drawing of the Magic Carpet; clay models of a jinrikisha, a Korean jiggy, a sedan chair, a Chinese wheelbarrow, a Chinese cart, an elephant with a howdah on his back, a caravan of camels, a Belgian dog-cart, etc.

Chapter 3. — This chapter should be enacted by two children, in costume if possible. The various methods of travel in Colonial days should be shown on the sand table: an Indian trail, a stream with stepping-stones and a log foot-bridge, a dugout, a birch-bark canoe with an Indian paddling it, a horse carrying two persons.

For the Museum: The objects modeled for the sand table; also pictures of Colonial coaches and taverns.

Chapter 4. — The children should make an excursion on foot into the country. The roadside game described in the text may be the basis for a project connected with composition. Stories of other walking expeditions made by the individual children may prove interesting.

For the Museum: Photographs and clay models showing walking scenes in places where no other form of transportation is practical, such as a camping trip in Africa, mountain climbing in the Alps, portage of a canoe in the woods; a Boy Scout; a soldier on march.

Chapter 5. — Such members of the class as have had actual experience should tell of their rides in horse-drawn sleighs. A snow scene may be arranged on the sand table showing the different means of travel described in the text. Additional stories of dog heroes of the Far North should be told in class.

For the Museum: The objects used in the snow scene above: a sled, a horse-drawn sleigh, Dutch ice-skaters, a ski-jumper, a reindeer sled with Eskimo driver, an Alaskan dog-sled and team.

Chapter 6. — If possible an excursion should be made to a farm in the country near by. A farm scene may be shown on the sand table. Special stress should be laid on the work done by horses in transporting farm produce.

For the Museum: Photographs or models of a horse, an ancient chariot, Paul Revere, an ox, a mule, old-fashioned carriages, a barn yard scene, an early settler's cart, a covered wagon, a stage coach, a hansom cab, a pony.

Chapter 7. — A bicycle should be brought into the schoolroom, so that it

may be examined in detail by the children. An excursion to a local bicycle and motor cycle dealer should be arranged.

For the Museum: Drawings of the first bicycles, and photographs of late models of bicycles and motor cycles cut from magazines. Perhaps some of the children may be able to bring from home photographs of their grandmothers in bicycling costumes.

Chapters 8 and 9. — The legendary episode of the discovery of steam by Jamie Watt may be reënacted in the classroom. A small metal teakettle and an alcohol lamp are the only properties needed. The mechanism of the steam engine should be explained simply by means of a model or simple drawings. A trip to the local railroad station should be taken, and, if possible, arrangements should be made with the station superintendent to allow the children to inspect a Pullman sleeper. Special emphasis should be laid on the importance of the railroad freight service. The process of building a new railroad may be graphically worked out upon the sand table.

For the Museum: Models, photographs, and drawings of railroad trains of the past and the present; a map showing the chief railroad systems of the United States. Interesting material may perhaps be secured from the publicity departments of the larger railroads.

Chapter 10. — The trips on the street car and the motor bus, as described in the text, should be made by the children.

For the Museum: Photographs and toy models of street cars, motor busses, and taxicabs.

Chapter 11. — This chapter may be dramatized, three boys playing the rôles of Mr. Thomas, Mr. Richards, and Mr. Henry, each describing one of the methods of city transportation listed in this chapter.

For the Museum: Photographs of the elevated railway, the subway, and the Holland Tunnel cut from magazines and the pictorial sections of the newspapers; also pictures showing city streets crowded with traffic.

Chapters 12 and 13. — If possible, a short trip in automobiles should be arranged. The children should examine the different parts of an automobile, paying special attention to the engine and its mechanism. A miniature automobile show may be staged on the sand table, the models being cut from the advertisements of the current magazines. All the best known makes should be represented, and there should be samples of every type of car and truck. A safety first project should be worked out on the playground.

For the Museum: The exhibits from the sand table automobile show; a small toy automobile; a tiny doll dressed in duster and goggles to represent a motorist of the early days.

Chapter 14. — The two farms described in the text should be reproduced on the sand table to emphasize the prosperity brought by good roads. A concrete road may be laid on the sand table, the materials needed being a few pebbles, a little sand, and some Portland cement. These may be mixed with water and spread out on a roadbed. The desirability of dryness and durability in roads should be stressed. A tollgate of the past may also be made with little trouble.

For the Museum: Samples of concrete, asphalt, and the stones used in the various layers of a macadam road; a road map of the country that surrounds the children's home city; photographs of fine streets and roads, of the Lincoln Highway, or the Dixie Highway; small drawings of road markers, such as "Stop," "Slow," etc.

Chapter 15. — The pageant may be enacted in the classroom. The costumes are simple and the ship models may be made by the children themselves.

For the Museum: The ship models used in the play; also pictures of Neptune carrying his trident.

Chapter 16. — A miniature steamship hull should be laid down in the classroom to illustrate the general theory of ship building. The ribs and the keel may be painted steel gray and a covering of tinfoil will serve to represent the steel plates of the sides. During these lessons on ships, the hours and half-hours in the classroom may be sounded with bells, after the system on shipboard. (One bell for 12:30 A.M.; two bells for 1 A.M.; three bells for 1.30 A.M., etc. to eight bells, when we begin over again with one bell for 4:30 A.M., etc.)

For the Museum: Photographs showing as many different kinds of modern ships as possible, steamers, freighters, sailing vessels, motor ships, battleships, and submarines.

Chapter 17. — If possible, the children should be taken to view an airplane at close range. Lighter-than-air craft may be demonstrated in class with a child's gas-filled toy balloon.

For the Museum: Models of an airship and an airplane; pictures of the air heroes mentioned in the text; a modern city airport may be erected with cheap toy airplanes, and a tin toy garage transformed into a hangar with the name of the city printed upon it. The beacon light should not be forgotten.

Chapter 18. — A telegram from a distant friend should be sent to the Journey Club. The project of a visit to the telegraph office should be carried out as outlined. The various ways of sending messages by code with drums, with poles in the ground, and with smoke or fire signals, wigwagging and heliographing, are easily demonstrable upon the school playground.

For the Museum: The telegram that was sent to the class; the Journey Club name written on a card in the Morse Code; drawing of telegraph poles; pictures showing various phases of the telegraph service. These last may be had upon application to the local telegraph company.

Chapter 19. — A visit should be made to the central office of the local telephone company so that the children may see for themselves what happens when they telephone.

For the Museum: A toy telephone; a card upon which there are listed the many materials needed for the telephone; pictures of the telephone in use; graphic chart showing the relative number of telephones in the United States and in the great nations of Europe.

Chapter 20. — Arrangements should be made with one of the local radio stores for a radio demonstration in the classroom.

For the Museum: Pictures of various types of radio outfits; a model showing the tall towers above a radio broadcasting studio; the radio page of a local newspaper with its long lists of stations and programs.

WHAT THIS BOOK CONTAINS